"Professor Dryden's book offers students and practitioners of psychotherapy a unique opportunity to learn from transcripts of therapy sessions which he conducted with Indian clients. He demonstrates and elucidates problem assessment and solution using the RECBT model in his distinctive style, which is precise and thorough. It will help the readers to learn the nuances of applications of RECBT to a variety of client problems. These transcripts provide an excellent example of effective use of the therapeutic technique within the framework of a well-formed therapeutic alliance."

– **Swati Khanolkar**, Associate Fellow and Supervisor, Albert Ellis Institute, New York; Director, In Vivo-Mumbai Centre for RECBT

"For anyone who is interested in aspects of culture as they relate to problems of daily living in India, this book provides a window into how Rational Emotive Behaviour Therapy can be applied. As always, Dryden delivers a product that invites the reader to understand the necessity of adapting a therapeutic approach to meet the needs of the individual through his expertise, experience and unique style. By highlighting the significance of a focused assessment of each of the volunteer's adversity, Dryden demonstrates acumen in assisting each person he works with to overcome their problem efficiently and effectively in the context of their unique cultural framework. The combination of didactic teaching and verbatim transcripts affords the reader an in-depth perspective of the evolution of theory into practice. This book will not disappoint."

– **Kristene A. Doyle**, Ph.D., Director of the Albert Ellis Institute

Rational Emotive Behaviour Therapy in India

Rational Emotive Behaviour Therapy in India: Very Brief Therapy for Problems of Daily Living is the first book of its kind to look specifically at using Rational Emotive Behaviour Therapy (REBT) for helping people with problems that are common in India.

Based on training workshops given by Professor Windy Dryden in Mumbai, this book presents transcripts of the workshop sessions alongside professional commentary, followed by reflections from the volunteers themselves.

With the emphasis on everyday problems, and clear examples of how REBT is applied, *Rational Emotive Behaviour Therapy in India* will be essential reading for psychotherapists, students and other mental health professionals working in India, and anyone interested in the cross-cultural application of psychotherapy.

Windy Dryden is in clinical and consultative practice and is an international authority on Cognitive Behaviour Therapy. He is Emeritus Professor of Psychotherapeutic Studies at Goldsmiths, University of London. He has worked in psychotherapy for more than 40 years and is the author or editor of over 225 books.

Rational Emotive Behaviour Therapy in India

Very Brief Therapy for Problems of Daily Living

Windy Dryden

Routledge
Taylor & Francis Group

LONDON AND NEW YORK

First published 2019
by Routledge
2 Park Square, Milton Park, Abingdon, Oxon OX14 4RN

and by Routledge
52 Vanderbilt Avenue, New York, NY 10017

Routledge is an imprint of the Taylor & Francis Group, an informa business

British Library Cataloguing-in-Publication Data
A catalogue record for this book is available from the British Library

Library of Congress Cataloging-in-Publication Data
A catalog record has been requested for this book

ISBN: 978-0-367-18974-7 (hbk)
ISBN: 978-0-367-18975-4 (pbk)
ISBN: 978-0-429-19965-3 (ebk)

Typeset in Times New Roman
by Newgen Publishing UK

Contents

Introduction

The idea for this book developed while I was in Mumbai in November 2017 conducting some training workshops for Indian therapists, most of whom had had prior exposure to Rational Emotive Behaviour Therapy (henceforth referred to as REBT). During these training sessions, I conducted several live demonstrations of REBT which I recorded. Upon request, I later sent the volunteers a copy of the recording and the transcript for their review. It was put to me that it would be good to have a book on REBT specifically for the Indian market where the emphasis was on helping people with problems that were common in India and where readers could see REBT in action. I agreed to do this, and this book is the result.

I begin the book by discussing in Chapter 1 the nature of REBT and the ideas that I take from it that inform my practice in a single brief session of therapy[1]. In particular, I discuss how I, as an REBT practitioner, seek to understand my clients' problematic responses to the adversities that feature in their issues and how I conceptualise possible healthy alternative responses to the same adversities which may serve as the clients' goals going forward.

In Chapter 2, I focus on practice and what I strive to do in very brief single sessions of REBT. The way I work in these sessions is informed not only by REBT but by the ideas that have stemmed from the general field of single-session therapy and walk-in therapy (Hoyt, Bobele, Slive, Young & Talmon, 2018; Hoyt & Talmon, 2014 and Talmon, 1990). I make both clear in this chapter.

In Chapters 3–13, I present and discuss 11 sessions of REBT that I did with volunteers from the training sessions that I conducted as described earlier. Volunteers were asked to discuss a genuine problem for which they sought help and that they were prepared to discuss with me in front of a group of their peers. They later provided written permission to have the session included and discussed in this book. It should be noted at the outset that all the people who attended my training sessions were female and thus there are no sessions with men represented in the book. In each of these chapters, I not only present a verbatim transcript of the session, but I also provide a commentary of my work and make links with the material that I discussed in Chapters 1 and 2. Also, seven months after the conversation that they had with me, each volunteer was invited to contribute a short reflection on the conversation and what they got out of it. What they wrote appears at the end of the relevant chapter.

Finally, in Chapter 14, I provide some reflections and a summary of what I covered in the book and a tentative conclusion.

While a single session of therapy can last anywhere from 50 minutes to three hours (see Davis III, Ollendick & Öst, 2012) in clinical work, a very brief single therapeutic session where I demonstrate my work to an audience usually lasts for less than 30 minutes. Elsewhere, I have referred to such a session as a 'very brief therapeutic conversation' (VBTC) – see Dryden (2018a) – and I will use this acronym throughout this book.

In reading this book, please keep in mind that all the volunteers were attending a course on REBT. Some had also had prior training in this therapeutic approach, and most had indicated a wish to continue their training in REBT going forward. Given this, it is not an unreasonable assumption that they had some knowledge of REBT and were positively predisposed towards it. I was aware of this situation, and it may have had some influence on my work. However, I was also aware at the time thinking that I should still explain REBT concepts since the volunteer may not see its applicability to their problem or they may have doubts about using a particular concept to help themself. Thus, I assumed that while *in general*, a volunteer may know more about REBT than other volunteers who were not on REBT-based training courses, *in particular*, they may not understand how its concepts, as broadly understood, might be relevant for their problem and potential solution.

I hope you enjoy this book and find it rewarding. If you have any comments on this book that you would like to share with me, I would be happy to receive them at www.windydryden.com

Windy Dryden
July 2018
London & Eastbourne, UK

Note

1 If you are new to REBT and require a more thorough introduction to this approach to therapy than that which appears in this book, I recommend Matweychuk and Dryden (2017) and Joshi and Phadke (2018).

Chapter 1

Understanding problems of daily living and their possible solution

Contributions from Rational Emotive Behaviour Therapy

In this opening chapter, I will present the basics of Rational Emotive Behaviour Therapy (or REBT) as they contribute to an understanding of problems of daily living and their possible solution. In doing so, I will emphasise its features that are particularly relevant to REBT's practice in very brief therapeutic conversations (VBTCs) which is the focus of this book.

REBT's ABC framework

Perhaps one of the things that REBT is best known for is its ABC framework. I use this framework to help me to understand the problems of the people who volunteer to have a very brief therapeutic conversation (VBTC) with me and what might constitute solutions to these problems.

A = Adversity

Beck (1976) argued that it is important to understand people with respect to their personal domain. He said that 'the objects – tangible and intangible – in which a person has an involvement constitute his personal domain'. The more involvement the person has with one such object, the more central a place it occupies in their personal domain. Beck (1976: 56) went on to say that 'the nature of a person's emotional response – or emotional disturbance – depends on whether he perceives events as adding to, subtracting from, endangering or impinging upon his domain'. Therefore, the relationship between what happens to the person and their personal domain is key to understanding whether or not that event will be seen as an adversity. Given this relationship, an adversity is likely to be an inference (i.e. a hunch that the person makes about what has happened that may be accurate or inaccurate). As I will discuss in the next chapter, when working with a nominated problem, as an REBT therapist, I will frequently encourage the volunteer to assume temporarily that their inference is correct to enable them to identify their basic attitudes to the adversity that underpin their problematic responses to it. Common adversities that volunteers often discuss in VBTCs are shown in Appendix 1.

B = Basic attitude[1]

As a therapeutic approach, REBT sits most comfortably within the cognitive-behavioural therapeutic tradition. Loosely speaking, REBT agrees with Epictetus, the Stoic philosopher who famously said: 'What upsets people is not things themselves but their judgements about the things' (Epictetus, 1983: 13). My own REBT-based version of this quote is as follows: 'People are not disturbed by the adversities they face. Rather, they disturb themselves about these adversities by the rigid and extreme basic attitudes that they hold towards them'.

Why 'basic attitudes' and not 'beliefs'

Most REBT therapists use the more common term, 'beliefs', rather than 'basic attitudes' at 'B' in the 'ABC' framework. However, I prefer the term 'basic attitudes', since I find the term 'beliefs' problematic and confusing to clients and professionals alike (Dryden, 2013).

Thus, the term 'belief' has been defined by the *Oxford Dictionary of Psychology*, 4th edition (Colman, 2015) as 'any proposition that is accepted as true on the basis of inconclusive evidence'. For example, a person may say something like: 'I believe my boss criticised me' and while they think that they have articulated a belief, this is not a belief as the term is employed in REBT, but rather an inference. In REBT, it is very important to distinguish between an inference at 'A' and an attitude (or belief in the traditional REBT sense) at 'B' and anything that helps this distinction to be made routinely is to be welcomed. Using the term 'attitude' rather than 'belief' in REBT is one way of doing so.

Definitions of the term 'attitude' are closer to the meaning that REBT theorists ascribe to the term 'belief'. The one that I think best captures Ellis's ideas is as follows: 'an enduring pattern of evaluative responses towards a person, object, or issue' (Colman, 2015). Before I introduced this change of terminology, I used the term 'attitude' rather than 'belief' with my clients and found that it was easier for me to convey the meaning of 'B' when I used 'attitude' than when I used 'belief' and they, in general, found 'attitude' easier to understand in this context than 'belief'.

Consequently, in this book, I will use the term 'attitude' instead of the term 'belief' to denote an evaluative stance taken by a person towards an adversity at 'A' which has emotional, behavioural and thinking implications. In deciding to use the term 'attitude' rather than the term 'belief', I recognise that when it comes to explaining what the 'B' stands for in the ABC framework, the term 'attitude' is problematic because it begins with the letter 'A'. Rather than use an 'AAC' framework which is not nearly as catchy or as memorable as the 'ABC' framework, I now use the phrase 'Basic Attitude'[2] when formally describing 'B' in the ABC framework. While not ideal, this term includes the word 'attitudes' and indicates that they are central or basic in that they lie at the base of a person's responses to an adversity.

In using the word 'basic', I have thus preserved the letter 'B' so that the well-known 'ABC' framework can be used. However, throughout the book when not formally describing the 'ABC' framework I will employ the word 'attitude' rather than the phrase 'basic attitude' when referring to the particular kind of cognitive processing that REBT argues mediates between an adversity and the person's responses to that negative event.

I will now discuss the types of (basic) attitudes that underpin both a person's disturbed response to an adversity and their healthy response to the same adversity.

Rigid and extreme basic attitudes

I mentioned earlier my REBT-reformulation of Epictetus's famous quote: 'What upsets people is not things themselves but their judgements about the things' (Epictetus, 1983: 13). If you recall, this reformulation was, 'People are not disturbed by the adversities they face. Rather, they disturb themselves about these adversities by the rigid and extreme basic attitudes that they hold towards them'. While this reformulation stresses the central importance of rigid and extreme basic attitudes in accounting for psychological disturbance, Ellis (e.g. 1994) long argued that rigidity is at the very core of such disturbance with extreme basic attitudes being derived from this core.

RIGID ATTITUDES

A rigid attitude is based on the person's desire for something to occur or not occur (e.g. "I want my readers to like this book"). When the person holds a rigid attitude, they then demand that they get their desired condition met (e.g. "I want my readers to like this book, and therefore they have to do so"). When the person holds a rigid attitude they are trying to exclude the possibility (either in their mind and / or in reality) that the desired condition will not occur (I will refer to this henceforth as an adversity).

EXTREME ATTITUDES

REBT theory posits that when a person holds a rigid attitude towards an adversity, then when they face the adversity in life or in imagination they will hold one or more of the following extreme attitudes: i) awfulising attitudes; ii) discomfort intolerance attitudes and iii) devaluation attitudes.

Awfulising attitudes   An awfulising attitude is based on a negative evaluation of the context in which the adversity occurred (e.g. "It would be bad if my readers did not like my book"). When the person holds an awfulising attitude, they then take this negative evaluation and make it extreme (e.g. "It would be bad if my readers did not like my book and therefore it would be awful"). When the person holds an awfulising attitude, they think at the time that nothing could be worse and that their life would be irredeemable if the adversity occurred.

Discomfort intolerance attitudes   A discomfort intolerance attitude is based on the person's view that it would be a struggle for them to tolerate the discomfort involved if the adversity occurred (e.g. "It would be hard for me to tolerate it if my readers did not like my book"). When the person holds a discomfort intolerance attitude, they then take this struggle and make it extreme (e.g. "It would be hard for me to tolerate it if my readers did not like my book and therefore it would be intolerable"). When the person holds a discomfort intolerance attitude, they think at the time that they do not have the resources to withstand the adversity and that they would in some way collapse irretrievably in the face of it.

While they overlap, a discomfort intolerance attitude differs from an awfulising attitude in that in the former the person's focus is on their ability to withstand the discomfort associated with the presence of the adversity while in the latter their focus is on an evaluation of the context in which the adversity occurred. As they are closely associated, a person will often have both, although one would usually be more to the fore than the other.

Devaluation attitudes   Like an awfulising attitude, a devaluation attitude is based on a negative evaluation. In this case, the person makes a negative evaluation of an aspect of self, other or life or of an experience that the person has faced (e.g. "It would be bad if my readers did not like my book"). When the person holds a devaluation attitude, they then take this negative evaluation of a part, aspect or experience and make it extreme by evaluating the whole of self, other or life depending upon whom or what the person holds responsible for the evaluated part, aspect or experience. For example, "It would be bad if my readers did not like my book and if this happens it proves that I am useless as both a writer and a person". When the person holds a devaluation attitude, they make what is known as the part-whole illogical error.

Flexible and non-extreme basic attitudes

The following quote sums up REBT's position on psychologically healthy responses to adversity: 'People respond healthily to adversity when they hold a set of flexible and non-extreme attitudes towards the adversity that they face'. Ellis (e.g. 1994) argued that flexibility is at the very core of psychological health with non-extreme basic attitudes being derived from this core.

FLEXIBLE ATTITUDES

Like a rigid attitude, a flexible attitude is based on the person's desire for something to occur or not occur (e.g. "I want my readers to like this book"). When the person holds a flexible attitude, they do not demand that they get their desired condition met (e.g. "I want my readers to like this book, but that does not mean that they have to do so"). When the person holds a flexible attitude towards an adversity, they accept that it may occur.

NON-EXTREME ATTITUDES

REBT theory posits that when a person holds a flexible attitude towards an adversity, then when they face the adversity in life or in imagination they will hold one or more of the following non-extreme attitudes: i) non-awfulising attitudes; ii) discomfort tolerance attitudes and iii) acceptance attitudes.

Non-awfulising attitudes   As with an awfulising attitude, a non-awfulising attitude is again based on a negative evaluation of the context in which the adversity occurred (e.g. "It would be bad if my readers did not like my book"). When the person holds a non-awfulising attitude, they keep this negative evaluation non-extreme (e.g. "It would be bad if my readers did not like my book, but it would not be awful"). In doing so, they recognise that things could be worse and that their life would be redeemable if the adversity occurred.

Discomfort tolerance attitudes   Like a discomfort intolerance attitude, a discomfort tolerance attitude is based on the person's view that it would be a struggle for them to tolerate the discomfort involved if the adversity occurred (e.g. "It would be hard for me to tolerate it if my readers did not like my book"). When the person holds a discomfort tolerance attitude, they focus on this struggle and keep it non-extreme (e.g. "It would be hard for me to tolerate it if my readers did not like my book, but it would be intolerable. I can tolerate it if it is worth it to me to do so and if this is the case, I am willing to do so and will commit myself to so doing"). This means that they think at the time that they have the resources to withstand the adversity and that they would in no way collapse irretrievably.

Unconditional acceptance attitudes   Like a devaluation attitude, an unconditional acceptance attitude is based on a negative evaluation. Again, in this case, the person makes a negative evaluation of an aspect of self, other or life or of an experience that the person has faced (e.g. "It would be bad if my readers did not like my book"). When the person holds an unconditional attitude, they then take this negative evaluation of a part, aspect or experience and keep it non-extreme by unconditionally accepting the whole of self, other or life depending upon whom or what the person holds responsible for the evaluated part, aspect or experience. For example, "It would be bad if my readers did not like my book and if this happens, it proves that I am fallible, unique, in flux and too complex to rate myself". When the person holds an unconditional acceptance attitude, they refrain from making the part-whole illogical error. Rather, they recognise that the whole incorporates the part and that the whole cannot legitimately be rated.

C = Consequences

So far, I have discussed the 'A' and 'B' parts of the ABC model. In particular, I have taken the situation where 'A' is a negative event that I have referred to as an adversity[3]. In doing so, I have shown that the person has a choice to process this adversity with rigid and extreme attitudes or with flexible and non-extreme attitudes. The former underpins a psychologically disturbed response to the adversity, while the latter underpins a psychologically healthy response to the same adversity[4]. In this section, I will take each of these responses in turn.

Unhealthy consequences

When a volunteer seeks help for a problem, it is because they are in emotional pain or because they are acting in ways that are self-defeating or relationship-defeating. These are seen in REBT as emotional and behavioural consequences of a set of basic attitudes that are rigid and extreme in the face of adversity as discussed earlier. The emotional consequences of rigid / extreme attitudes are deemed to be negative in experiential tone and unhealthy in their effects and are known in REBT as unhealthy negative emotions (UNEs). Correspondingly, the behavioural consequences of these rigid / extreme attitudes are deemed to be unconstructive or dysfunctional. Modern REBT also recognises that there are cognitive consequences ('C') of these rigid / extreme attitudes (at 'B') which can be verbal or visual (Dryden, 2016). These cognitions take the form of highly distorted inferences about the adversity and related matters and are skewed to the negative. They are usually far more distorted than the inferences that the person makes at 'A'. Also, such cognitions tend to be ruminative in nature.

Healthy consequences

When I help the volunteer to deal more effectively with the adversity at 'A', it is because I have encouraged them to develop and hold a set of basic attitudes towards the same adversity that are flexible and non-extreme. The emotional consequences of flexible / non-extreme attitudes like their rigid / extreme counterparts are also deemed to be negative in experiential tone, but this time they are healthy in their effects. In REBT, these are known as healthy negative emotions (HNEs). Correspondingly, the behavioural consequences of these flexible / extreme attitudes are deemed to be constructive or functional. Again, modern REBT also recognises that there are cognitive consequences ('C') of these flexible / non-extreme attitudes (at 'B') which also can be verbal or visual (Dryden, 2016). These cognitions take the form of realistic inferences about the adversity and related matters and are balanced in nature. They are usually non-ruminative in nature.

The emotional, behavioural and cognitive consequences ('C') of both rigid / extreme and flexible / non-extreme basic attitudes held at 'B' towards a variety of adversities at 'A' are shown in Appendix 1. I will discuss this further later.

I have now discussed REBT's ABC model in general terms. This is the framework that guided me when I was working in a very brief manner with the volunteers whose sessions are presented and discussed in Chapters 3–13. Let me now discuss this framework as it applies to a range of emotional problems for which people (including the volunteers discussed in this book) seek help and what might constitute solutions to these problems.

Understanding problematic responses to adversity

When a person seeks help for a problem within the context of a very brief therapeutic conversation that will last for less than 30 minutes, it is important for me to have an accurate understanding of that problem. In doing so, I use REBT's ABC framework, as discussed earlier, which offers me a way of understanding what they find particularly troublesome in their nominated problem (i.e. the adversity at 'A') and what are their problematic responses (at 'C') to this adversity. In discussing this subject here, I refer the reader to Appendix 1 which outlines the 'ABCs' of the eight major troublesome emotions for which people seek therapeutic help (i.e. anxiety, depression, guilt, shame, hurt and the problematic forms of anger, jealousy and envy).

Anxiety

From an REBT perspective, a person experiences anxiety (at 'C') when they infer the presence of an imminent threat to an important aspect of their personal domain (at 'A') which they evaluate with rigid and extreme attitudes (at 'B'). In the clinical literature, there are a number of so-called 'anxiety disorders' which, from an REBT perspective, can be understood with reference to the ABC model. Thus, in social anxiety disorder, the person is anxious (at 'C') about falling short of a socially based standard, thinking that this will be noticed by others who will judge them (at 'A'). In health anxiety, the person is anxious (at 'C') about uncertainty related to a threat to their health or well-being (at 'A') and in achievement anxiety, the person is anxious (at 'C') about a threat to a standard that they have set for themself concerning a task or set of tasks (at 'A'). In all these situations, the person experiences anxiety not because they encounter such threats but because they evaluate these threats with rigid and extreme attitudes at 'B'.

HOW A PERSON UNWITTINGLY MAINTAINS ANXIETY

In addition to holding rigid and extreme attitudes, the person maintains their anxiety in a number of ways. As an REBT therapist, working very briefly with a volunteer, I not only want to understand how the person creates their anxiety, I also want to discover how they unwittingly maintain their anxiety. I say 'unwittingly' here because although the person *intends* to deal with their anxiety, the *effect* is anxiety maintenance. Examples are steps that they may take to prevent themself from experiencing anxiety in the first place and those they may take to rid themself of anxiety once they have begun to experience it.

Unless I help the person to deal with these maintenance factors, I will not have helped them to get the most out of the brief session for which they have volunteered. These factors can be behavioural or cognitive in nature (see Appendix 1). The main behavioural maintenance factors are what are known as safety-seeking behaviours the most common of which is avoidance. As can also be seen in Appendix 1 there are two different cognitive consequences in anxiety: threat exaggerating and safety-seeking. The person may alternate between the two. The effect of these maintenance factors is that they prevent the person from facing a threat long enough to enable them to process it fully.

Depression

From an REBT perspective, a person experiences depression (at 'C') when they infer the presence of loss, failure or undeserved plight (to self and / or others) in their personal domain (at 'A') which they evaluate with rigid and extreme attitudes (at 'B').

There are two personality dimensions which are regarded as risk factors for depression: autonomous and sociotropic.

AUTONOMOUS DEPRESSION

In autonomous depression, the person is particularly vulnerable to loss of autonomy (broadly defined) and personal weakness. This is why such individuals experience 'double-dose' depression. Thus, a person may become depressed about losing the role of the major family provider on being made redundant. Then the person may become further depressed because they regard depression as a sign of personal weakness. In both cases, it is important to remember the central mediating role of rigid and extreme attitudes held towards such loss and weakness.

SOCIOTROPIC DEPRESSION

In sociotropic depression, the person is particularly vulnerable to loss of interpersonal connection with valued others. Again, the mediating role of rigid and extreme attitudes towards this loss is crucial to consider.

HOW A PERSON UNWITTINGLY MAINTAINS DEPRESSION

Depression is created by the person holding rigid and extreme attitudes and often leads to the person withdrawing from previously rewarding activities and from people whom the person has previously found supportive. In this withdrawn and solitary state, the person often ruminates and elaborates on the negative meaning that they have given to the loss, failure or undeserved plight with the result that this negativity is increased with the concomitant deepening of depressed affect. For more information see Appendix 1.

Guilt

From an REBT perspective, a person experiences guilt (at 'C') when they consider that they have broken their moral code, failed to live up to their moral code or have hurt someone (at 'A') which they evaluate with rigid and extreme attitudes (at 'B'). Some people in the field consider that while shame involves judgements of the 'self', guilt involves judgements of one's behaviour (Tangney, 1995). However, I disagree. My view is that both shame and guilt involve self-judgements, but that the content of these judgements differs. In guilt, the person judges themself as 'bad' or similar variant, whereas in shame they judge themselves as defective or similar variant (see below).

HOW A PERSON UNWITTINGLY MAINTAINS GUILT

In addition to holding rigid and extreme attitudes, people who have a particular problem with guilt tend to assume too much responsibility for the outcome of their actions and assign too little responsibility to others involved. Once they feel guilty, they will either avoid reminders of what they have done or beg for forgiveness, which, even if given, will only provide relief for a short period.

Shame

From an REBT perspective, a person experiences shame when they have fallen very short of their ideal, and they think that others have judged them negatively for it. They also experience shame when a reference group with whom they identify falls very short of that group's ideal. They evaluate these adversities with rigid and extreme attitudes. In shame, the person judges themself as defective (as noted earlier), but they can also judge themself as disgusting or diminished.

HOW A PERSON UNWITTINGLY MAINTAINS SHAME

In addition to holding rigid and extreme attitudes, people who have a particular problem with shame avoid those whom they think will trigger their shame and they will also avoid places for the same reason. People with shame problems are often ambivalent about seeking help. While part of them wants to deal with their shame, another part of them feels ashamed of not being able to solve their problem on their own, thus leading them to be ambivalent about being helped.

Hurt

From an REBT perspective, a person feels hurt about two main adversities. First, they feel hurt about a situation where someone they care about is not as invested in their relationship as they are and they thought that both were equally invested. Second, they feel hurt about interpersonal adversities where they think that they have been treated badly by those to whom they feel close and where they think that they have not deserved such treatment by the other. As before, the person's hurt feelings stem from their rigid and extreme attitudes towards these adversities.

There are two types of hurt. Following the ideas of Howard Young (see Dryden, 1989), I call these types, 'less me' hurt and 'poor me' hurt. While the rigid attitudes tend to be the same in both types of hurt, the extreme attitudes are different.

In 'less me' hurt, the person concludes that the way they have been treated by the other means that they have less worth than they would have if they had been treated well. For example, "I have been left out of my friendship group which absolutely should not have happened and because it has, I am unlovable". In this type of hurt, therefore, the person's main extreme attitude is self-devaluation.

In 'poor me' hurt, the person's worth is not implicated, but they tend to see themself as a victim of undeserved treatment from the other. Their common rigid attitude is as before (i.e. "I have been left out of my friendship group which absolutely should not have happened"). However, their main extreme attitude is either i) an awfulising attitude (e.g. "It is awful to have been left out of my friendship group"); ii) a discomfort intolerance attitude (e.g. "I can't bear being left out of my friendship group") or iii) a life-devaluation attitude (e.g. "Life sucks for allowing me to be left out of my friendship group"). Each of these extreme attitudes leads the person to conclude 'poor me'.

HOW A PERSON UNWITTINGLY MAINTAINS HURT

In addition to holding rigid and extreme attitudes towards the above adversities, people who have a particular problem with hurt do not communicate their feelings to the other person involved. They tend to think that the other person caused their hurt feelings and correspondingly tend not to take responsibility for creating their own feelings. This is particularly the case with 'poor me' hurt.

Problematic anger

From an REBT perspective, a person feels angry when i) they think that they have been frustrated in some way or their movement towards an important goal has been obstructed; ii) someone has treated them badly; iii) someone has transgressed one of their personal rules; iv) they have transgressed one of their own personal rules and v) someone or something has threatened their self-esteem or disrespected them. When their anger is problematic, it is usually because it is unhealthy for the person themself and for other people involved, even though the person may not see this. Problematic anger stems from the rigid and extreme attitudes that the person holds towards the above adversities. It tends to be ad hominem, and when directed at other people, these people respond with their own problematic anger or with fear.

HOW A PERSON UNWITTINGLY MAINTAINS PROBLEMATIC ANGER

In addition to holding rigid and extreme attitudes towards the adversities listed earlier, people who have a particular problem with anger maintain it in a number of ways. First, they may not see that their anger is a problem for them. Indeed, often people with problematic anger say that they feel powerful or energised when they experience it or express it. Second, problematic anger, when expressed, may even get them what they want, at least in the short-term. Thus, expressed problematic anger often leads to compliance in fearful individuals. Also, in problematic anger, the person devalues the other, and in doing so, they may value themself more or distract themself temporarily from their self-devaluation. This is particularly the case in what some refer to as 'ego-defensive anger'.

Problematic jealousy

From an REBT perspective, a person experiences jealousy when they face or think they face a threat posed by a third person to the relationship that they have (or think they have) with someone close to them. In addition, they also struggle with jealousy when there is a threat posed by the uncertainty they face concerning their partner's whereabouts, behaviour or thinking in the context of the first threat. When jealousy is problematic, it is based on a set of rigid and extreme attitudes that the person holds towards one or both threats outlined above. In particular, the person's extreme attitudes are intolerability of threat-related uncertainty and self-devaluation. In the latter, if a threat is posed, then the person holds that they are bound to lose any resultant contest and that nobody else would be interested in them in the future. If nobody else would want them, then the person holds that this is another reason why they have to safeguard what they have and, of course, this means that they are oversensitive to the threat of its loss.

HOW A PERSON UNWITTINGLY MAINTAINS PROBLEMATIC JEALOUSY

In addition to holding rigid and extreme attitudes towards the two adversities listed earlier, and given that these adversities are threat-related, people unwittingly perpetuate the problematic form of their jealousy in ways similar to how they unwittingly perpetuate their anxiety. Thus, in seeking to protect themself from interpersonal threat, the person seeks to restrict the movements of their partner so that the latter does not meet other people that the person finds threatening. If the person cannot prevent the possible existence of such interpersonal threat, then they will scan their environment for it and then take steps to eliminate it once they perceive it or to get reassurance that no threat is posed. In seeking to protect themself from the uncertainty-related threat, the person will do all they can to gain certainty that the threat does not exist. For example, they will seek reassurance that no threat is posed, they will check on the person's whereabouts or they will set tests that the person has to pass. If their partner responds to such problem-related behaviour, then the partner is also unwittingly helping to maintain the person's problem with jealousy. However, if the person cannot convince themself that a threat does not exist to their relationship, then they will think that it does, given the fact that the person finds it very difficult to say, "I am not sure if a threat exists to my relationship, but it probably doesn't". The person's rigidity about the twin threats in jealousy explains why the person tends to see threat when none is likely to exist.

Problematic envy

From an REBT perspective, a person experiences envy when another possesses and enjoys something desirable that the first person does not have, but wants. When envy is problematic, it is based on a set of rigid and extreme attitudes that the person holds towards this adversity. In general, the person thinks i) that their worth as a person is based on what they have and if they lack something desirable than this means that they are less worthy than they would be if they possessed the desideratum and / or ii) that deprivation is intolerable and must be rectified immediately.

HOW A PERSON UNWITTINGLY MAINTAINS PROBLEMATIC ENVY

In addition to holding rigid and extreme attitudes towards not having what another person has and wanting to have it, the person unwittingly maintains their problematic envy, by acting on their 'need' to possess what they lack. They may spend an inordinate amount of time and effort trying to get what they 'need' and if and when they get the needed 'object' their joy and excitement is short-lived because a new adversity of lack will soon intrude into their life. Also, if they cannot get what they think they need, then they may 'equalise' the situation by spoiling the object for the person in real life or by denigrating it when discussing the issue with other people or when thinking about the situation in their own mind.

Because 'envy' can be a difficult emotion to admit to having, the person may deny that they have a problem because they would feel ashamed if they did. However, even if they do admit to having a problem with envy, they may continue to solve this psychological problem by non-psychological means (i.e. by acquiring the 'needed' object or possession) rather than by working to become flexible and non-extreme in their attitudes towards the envy-based adversity of lack.

Understanding healthy responses to adversity

In the same way as I use REBT's ABC framework to understand the dynamics of the person's problem, I also use it understand what is possible in the way of a realistic solution to the problem. In discussing this subject here, I refer the reader again to Appendix 1 which outlines the 'ABCs' of the eight major healthy alternatives to the troublesome emotions discussed earlier (i.e. concern, sadness, remorse, disappointment, sorrow and the non-problematic forms of anger, jealousy and envy). These are known in REBT as healthy negative emotions (HNEs) at 'C', and they stem from flexible and non-extreme attitudes towards adversities. In REBT theory, they are seen as qualitatively different from unhealthy negative emotions (UNEs) as they have different behavioural and cognitive associations at 'C' from UNEs (see Appendix 1). This means that a decrease in intensity of a UNE (e.g. less anxious) is still seen as a UNE since it will still have the same behavioural and cognitive associations as the more intense form of the emotion. On the other hand, an HNE alternative (such as concern as an alternative to anxiety) has different behavioural and cognitive associations at 'C'. Also, HNEs can be intense and healthy which is not possible in the 'quantitative' model of the emotions where a high-intensity negative emotion is seen as disturbed and the same emotion with lesser intensity is seen as healthy.

When discussing the HNEs in the following, it is important to note that the terminology that I use for each emotion is my own and some terms may not have meaning for volunteers. Thus, when applying such ideas with these people, I am more than happy to use terms that are meaningful to them rather than my own so long as they reflect the concept of HNEs.

Concern: The healthy alternative to anxiety

Concern when facing a threat to some important part of the person's personal domain is the healthy alternative to anxiety. When the person is feeling concerned, but not anxious, about the threat then they are facing the threat and processing it fully using flexible and non-extreme attitudes and without the use of safety-seeking behaviour and thinking. In REBT we argue that the best way to deal with anxiety problems is for the person to face a threat at 'A', develop a set of flexible and non-extreme attitudes towards this threat at 'B' and act and think in ways that support these attitudes.

The mindful position of acknowledging the presence of anxiety but neither engaging with it or distracting from it is important as is continuing to act towards values-based goals even when feeling anxious.

Sadness: The healthy alternative to depression

In REBT, we argue that the best way for the person to deal with problems of depression is for them to develop flexible and non-extreme attitudes towards loss, failure and undeserved plight as suffered by self and / or others. This will enable them to experience sadness rather than depression which will help them in a number of ways. First, it helps them to process the loss, failure or undeserved plight so that they can digest the adversity in healthy ways. Second, it helps the person to stay connected with people rather than withdraw from them. Finally, it helps the person to re-engage with pleasurable and meaningful activities.

Remorse: The healthy alternative to guilt

In REBT we argue that the best way for the person to deal with guilt problems is for them to face what they have done (or not done) at 'A' and develop a set of flexible and unconditional self-acceptance attitudes towards it at 'B'. This enables them to feel remorse, but not guilt about the adversity at 'A'. In doing so, they can place what they did in a more realistic context, realise that their action needs to be understood rather than being seen as equivalent to their identity. Then they need to act and think in ways that support these attitudes and related cognitions.

Disappointment: The healthy alternative to shame

In REBT, we argue that the best way for the person to deal with problems of shame is for them to develop flexible and unconditional self-acceptance attitudes when they have fallen very short of their ideal and others evaluate them negatively. This enables them to feel disappointment rather than shame. In particular, the person needs to practise the attitude of unconditional self-acceptance and be open about one's fallibilities with others.

Sorrow: The healthy alternative to hurt

In REBT, we argue that the best way for the person to deal with problems of hurt is for them to develop flexible and non-extreme attitudes towards situations where a) another person has invested less in their relationship than they have and where they thought that they were equally invested and b) others with whom they are close have treated them badly which they think they have not deserved.

It is important for the person to take responsibility for their own feelings and communicate their displeasure to the other for the way they treated the person. In doing so, their flexible and non-extreme attitudes will lead them to engage in an open-minded discussion about the matter where the person is open to the possibility that they may have in some way acted badly to the other preceding the other's bad behaviour towards them. Sorrow-based discussion thus often leads to the repair of interpersonal wounds and even the strengthening of interpersonal bonds.

Non-problematic anger: The healthy alternative to problematic anger

In REBT, we argue that anger can be healthy as well as unhealthy[5]. To deal with problematic anger, the person first needs to admit to themselves that their anger is problematic and that they need to change it. Then, they need to understand what they need to change it to – in this case, non-problematic anger. The therapist helps by clearly spelling out the features of non-problematic anger for the person. Thus, it is based on flexible and non-extreme attitudes towards anger-related adversities rather than on rigid and extreme attitudes. It is based on respect for the other rather than on other-devaluation. This other-respect encourages self-assertion, the aim of which is to communicate the person's feelings to the relevant other and to promote a healthy dialogue / discussion with that other. It may be necessary as well for the therapist to encourage the person to voice any doubts, reservations and objections (DROs) they have towards pursuing a non-problematic anger path and relinquishing the one based on problematic anger. These DROs and the misconceptions on which they are often based should then be discussed and dispelled.

Non-problematic jealousy: The healthy alternative to problematic jealousy

In REBT, we hold that jealousy can be healthy as well as unhealthy. When it is healthy, it is clear that the person is facing a threat to their relationship and is healthily concerned about this because they hold flexible and non-extreme attitudes towards this interpersonal threat. If it is not clear that a threat exists to the person's relationship with their partner then the person holds flexible and non-extreme attitudes towards this uncertainty-related threat, is able to tolerate such uncertainty and thus tends to think, "I am not sure if a threat exists to my relationship, but it probably doesn't".

Given that the person's attitude to self is not based on devaluation, they would be sad if they were to lose their partner but would tend to think that they would find someone else when they are ready to enter into a new relationship.

Non-problematic envy: The healthy alternative to problematic envy

In REBT, we hold that envy can be healthy as well as unhealthy. When it is healthy, the person focuses on what someone else has that they want but don't have and holds a set of flexible and non-extreme attitudes towards this adversity. Their flexible attitude helps them to stand back and question how much they want it and how much time and energy they are prepared to commit to obtaining it. This flexible attitude also helps them to think about what their life will be like with this desideratum and without it. Their unconditional self-acceptance, non-extreme attitude leads them to see that their worth remains the same whether or not they get what they want. Their discomfort tolerance attitude encourages them to put up with the discomfort involved with the deprivation of being without what they want.

When the other has what the person wants, but lacks a personal characteristic, skill or achievement, then non-problematic envy involves admiring and being pleased for the other. This healthy type of envy encourages the person to learn from the other and to use what they learn to pursue the desideratum if this will truly benefit the person's life or situation.

Summary

In this opening chapter, I have introduced the basic ideas of REBT, discussed each element of its ABC framework and shown how this framework can be used to understand both the problems of daily living that people have and seek help for and possible solutions to these problems. When discussing these problems, I specified eight unhealthy negative emotions (UNEs) that people experience and argued that a set of rigid and extreme attitudes towards a variety of adversities lie at the base of these problems. I then went on to discuss how people unwittingly maintain each of the UNEs listed that feature in their problems.

When discussing possible solutions to these problems of daily living, I argued that wherever possible, people should be helped to face adversity and learn to respond healthily to it. In doing so, I listed the eight healthy alternatives to the eight UNEs and referred to these as healthy negative emotions (HNEs). Such solutions are underpinned by the person holding a set of flexible and non-extreme attitudes towards adversity.

In the next chapter, I turn my attention to practice and show how I utilise REBT's concepts to help people address their problems of daily living within the context of a very brief therapeutic conversation.

Notes

1 In this book, the terms 'basic attitude' and 'attitude' will be used interchangeably.
2 As suggested by my good friend and colleague, Walter Matweychuk.
3 Of course, 'A' can also be a positive event, but as a person generally does not seek help when a positive event happens to them, unless they react to some negative aspect of the positive event, I will focus on the situation where 'A' is an adversity.
4 For a review of the evidence on this point see David, Cotet, Matu, Mogoase and Stefan (2018).
5 The subtitle of my book entitled 'Overcoming Anger' is, 'When Anger Helps and When It Hurts' (Dryden, 1996).

Chapter 2

The practice of REBT in very brief therapeutic conversations

In the opening chapter, I described the basics of REBT theory since it informs my understanding of a) the problems for which the volunteers seek my help within the context of very brief therapeutic conversations (VBTCs) and b) the possible solutions to these problems. In this chapter, I will consider what I as an REBT therapist can usefully offer volunteers in VBTCs and the main tasks that I have to perform in doing so. Before I begin, let me provide a reminder of the context in which the 11 conversations that appear in Chapters 3–13 took place. In November 2017, I was invited to give a series of workshops in India, and at every workshop, I gave a number of demonstrations of REBT with members of the audience related to the theme of the workshop. These volunteers, therefore, had an interest in REBT and most had received some prior training in it.

In what follows, I want to stress that the practical strategies and techniques described in this chapter should be regarded as therapeutic tools akin to tools in a maintenance person's toolkit. I have them with me, and I will use them when needed, but it is very unlikely that I will use every tool and certainly not on every occasion.

My goals as an REBT therapist in VBTCs

When a person volunteers to have a VBTC with me, I am mindful of the time that I have to help them. Thus, the range of the 11 conversations presented in this book was between 14 minutes 51 seconds and 25 minutes 32 seconds with a mean (average) length of 18 minutes 43 seconds. The most frequent length was just over 17 minutes. Given this, I have, roughly, half a regular 50-minute session to provide help to the volunteer. As such, I usually only have the time to help the person with one problem, although sometimes, if there is a linking theme (as with Maia in Chapter 5), I may be able to provide additional help.

When I ask for volunteers, I say something like:

> Please volunteer if you have a genuine, current emotional problem for which you would like help. A good problem to discuss would be one which, if solved, would make a difference to your life. Alternatively, it could be a problem with which you are stuck, and you would like to get unstuck so that you can move on in that particular area of your life.

When the person brings a problem, I see it that my basic goal is to help them to identify the key adversity in that problem and to encourage them to deal effectively with that adversity. As I discuss in greater detail later, this involves me encouraging the volunteer to work towards experiencing a healthy negative emotion (HNE) in response to the adversity, and then to change the adversity if it can be changed, or to adjust constructively to it if it cannot be changed. If I have time and it is appropriate, I also strive to help the volunteer to generalise what they have learned from our conversation about their nominated problem to other similar problems. I have written elsewhere (Dryden, 2019) that one of the things that I have learned from my work as a single-session therapist is to curb my inclination to give people too many 'pearls of wisdom' to take home with them. On the basis of 'less is more', if I can help the volunteer to take away from our conversation one thing that might make a significant difference to them as they address their problem in their own life, then I consider that I have achieved my main goal as an REBT therapist in VBTCs (see Keller & Papasan, 2012).

My other goal in conducting VBTCs is to help the volunteer to have realistic expectations of what they can achieve from the process. It is rare that a volunteer experiences a profound change in personality[1] as a result of having a short conversation with me about their problem and what they can do about it. On the other hand, some people do report that they have made lasting changes as a direct result of having a VBTC with me (Dryden, 2018a). If the conditions are right and both the volunteer and myself are prepared to roll up our sleeves and get down to business then realistic, but meaningful, change is possible.

The case of 'Vera'

Let me demonstrate what a person can do in a short period of time from therapy when they put their mind to it by discussing the case of 'Vera'. Vera sought therapy from Dr Albert Ellis, the founder of REBT, for help with an elevator phobia. Because she could not afford his individual therapy, Ellis suggested that Vera joined one of his groups which she did. In the group, Ellis outlined how to address an elevator phobia which involves riding in elevators while tolerating the feelings of anxiety and doing so repeatedly until the person is no longer anxious. No matter what Ellis and the other group members did, Vera would not do this, but always had a 'good' reason why she could not do so.

This went on for about two years until one Friday afternoon Vera requested another individual session with Ellis, desperate for help. The reason was that she had just been informed earlier that day that the office where she worked was moving over the weekend from the fifth floor of the building where it was located to the 105th floor of the same building.

She told Ellis that she had to get over her problem by Monday morning since while she could just about walk up five floors, she could not walk up 105 floors and she needed the job. Ellis told her that she knew what she needed to do which, as it transpired, she did. She spent the weekend going up and down elevators while tolerating her anxiety until she could ride an elevator unanxiously.

Four conditions for rapid change

VBTCs are based on the idea that the volunteer is capable of helping themself quickly and can maintain this change. For the volunteer to initiate self-help quickly, four important conditions need to be present: i) knowledge; ii) a committed reason to change; iii) taking appropriate action and iv) preparedness to accept the costs of change if any. If all four ingredients are present, then the person will be able to initiate change in a short period. Let me deal with these conditions one at a time.

Knowing what to do to change

It is important that a person has some understanding of what they need to do to change. As we have seen, Vera had an elevator phobia and knew that to deal constructively with this problem she had to ride on elevators frequently. This knowledge was necessary, but insufficient for Vera to change since although she knew what to do for a long time, she did not do it and therefore did not change.

Having a committed reason to change

Unless the person has a reason to change and this reason is important for the person then the person will probably not change. Vera never really had to use elevators. The office where she worked was on the fifth floor of a building, and she was able to walk up five flights of stairs. Thus, for two years she flirted with the idea of change but did not do so. When the office moved to the 105th floor she had a committed reason to change because she needed to keep her job. Effectively, she had to change over the weekend, or she was out of a job.

Taking appropriate action

A person may have a committed reason to change, but unless they take appropriate action, then change won't happen. Vera took action by taking many elevator rides over a short period. If she had not, she would not have addressed her problem effectively.

Being prepared to accept the costs of personal change, if any

Change is often painful. It involves some discomfort and may involve the loss of certain benefits. If the person is not prepared to accept these costs, then they will soon stop taking appropriate action discussed earlier, and any change that they may have made may well evaporate. Vera was prepared to tolerate the considerable discomfort that she experienced while embarking on her exposure programme.

My therapeutic tasks in VBTCs

As I have made clear, I see it that my major role as an REBT therapist is to help the volunteer to deal with whatever problem they wish to discuss with me. For me to be of any help, their problem needs to be genuine, current and one that they wish to solve now. Given this context, I will now outline my major tasks in helping the volunteer with their problem.

Adopting a problem-focused approach at the outset

As you will see from the conversations that I present in Chapters 3–13, I begin each conversation in the same way with some variant of "What problem can I help you with today?". I see REBT as an approach to VBTCs (Dryden, 2018a) and single-session therapy (Dryden, 2019) that is both problem-focused and goal-oriented. My view is that I am best placed to help the volunteer achieve a realistic problem-related goal once I have understood the nature of that problem.

Selecting and working with a target problem

It sometimes happens when I ask the volunteer for a problem that they tell me that they have more than one. If that happens, I explain that we only have time to deal with one problem and invite them to select one which I will henceforth refer to as the target problem. However, I also explain that if possible I will suggest ways that they may be able to generalise what they have learned from discussing their target problem to other problems.

Working with a specific example of the target problem

Whenever possible, it is useful for myself and the volunteer to work with a specific example of the target problem. The reason for this is that such an example provides the specific information that we both need to find a meaningful solution to the client's problem. Thus, a specific example takes place in a specific situation, with specific people present acting in specific ways. A specific example of the target problem may be typical, vivid and / or currently on the person's mind. It may have occurred in the past or may occur in the near future. There is particular value in selecting an imminent example of the target problem to work with because the person can then apply what they have learned from discussing this example with me to the same situation in the very near future.

Understanding the target problem in context

Although the time that I have with the volunteer in a VBTC is strictly limited, I have found it valuable to let the volunteer talk a little about the target problem so that I can understand it in context. This will be apparent in virtually all the conversations that appear in Chapters 3–13. Understanding the problem in context involves me asking questions to enable the person to clarify this context so that the real problem emerges more readily. Without this context, the volunteer may select a problem which may not get to the heart of what they are most troubled about.

Assessing the target problem

When I assess the volunteer's target problem, I use REBT's ABC framework which I discussed in detail in Chapter 1. While I may use this framework formally with a volunteer, more often I use it to guide my interventions and will not necessarily refer to the problem-related ABC framework explicitly. Let me briefly provide a reminder of each of the elements of this framework when assessing the person's problem:

'A' stands for 'adversity' which is the aspect of the situation that the person is most disturbed about

'B' stands for the rigid and / extreme basic attitude that the person holds towards the adversity and which largely accounts for this disturbance

'C' stands for the emotional, behavioural and cognitive consequences of the above basic attitude. Given that the person has a problem then they will tend to have an unhealthy negative emotional response to the adversity, act in an unconstructive way and subsequently have thoughts that are highly distorted, skewed to the negative and ruminative.

When I come to assess the person's target problem, then I will assess 'A' and 'C' before 'B' since when the volunteer talks about their problem, they will either discuss their disturbed responses (at 'C') and what they are disturbed about (at 'A') rather than the basic attitudes that give rise to the disturbance. Whether I will assess 'A' before 'C' or vice versa will depend on in which order the volunteer discusses these factors. Here, I will discuss the issues that relate to assessing 'C' before considering those that relate to assessing 'A'.

As I am likely to assess a specific example of the volunteer's problem, I will first gain some understanding of the situation in which this problem example took place. Thus, as noted earlier, it is useful for me to know where the problem was experienced, who was present and what they did that was relevant to the person's problem. Maultsby (1975) referred to this as the 'camera check' in that it is what a camera with an audio channel would have recorded of what happened.

Assessing 'C'

When assessing 'C', as noted earlier, I want to know my client's major unhealthy negative emotion (UNE) and their accompanying unconstructive behaviour. If relevant, and I have time, I also want to discover what the thinking consequences of their rigid and extreme attitudes are.

Assessing the emotional 'C'

Here, I want to identify the volunteer's major UNE. So, if they give me several such emotions, I can ask them to nominate i) the one emotion that best encapsulates their problem; ii) the emotion they find most troubling or iii) the emotion they want to tackle first. In Appendix 1, I outline the eight major UNEs for which people seek help, and I have this list in mind when helping the volunteer to identify their target UNE at 'C'.

I normally encounter two problems when assessing the emotional 'C'. First, the person may give me a vague emotion. Thus, they may say that they felt 'bad' or 'upset' in response to my enquiry. If they do, I will explain why such a response is vague and ask them again to give me a specific UNE. I may even list the eight UNEs and ask them to pick the one with best describes their emotional response.

Second, the person may give me an inference and not an emotion. For example, the person may say, "I felt rejected" or "I felt ignored". As can be seen, these are inferences and not emotions. If this happens, I explain the phenomenon and ask for their major disturbed emotion about their inference (e.g. "How did you feel about being rejected?").

Example. In outlining the practice of VBTC, I will discuss a typical problem that a person may wish to discuss with me. Unlike the conversations that I will present in Chapters 3–13, the example that I will discuss here is a composite one drawn from a number of different VBTCs that I have over the years. The person, whom I shall call Saisha, has a social anxiety problem.

Assessing the behavioural 'C'

Once I have identified the volunteer's major UNE, I often ask them to tell me about their accompanying unconstructive behaviour. This may be behaviour that is an expression of the emotion, or it may be behaviour designed to help the person get rid of or distract themself from the troublesome emotion. As such, it is important for me to encourage the volunteer to set a constructive behavioural goal in the goal-setting stage of the conversation.

Example. When Saisha experiences social anxiety she stays silent or withdraws from the situation she is in, if she can.

Assessing the cognitive 'C'

In some problems like anxiety, the person unwittingly creates highly distorted thinking from their rigid and extreme attitudes towards the adversity which they then respond to in a way that maintains their problem. See an example of this in Chapters 12 and 13. For example, I may say, "Once your anxiety took root, what thoughts did you have about the adversity and your ability to cope with it?"

Example. When Saisha was in the midst of anxiety, she subsequently thought that the people she was with would always think she was a weirdo.

Assessing 'A'

One of the reasons that I like to have a clear idea of what happened in the situation in which the volunteer experienced their problem is that I will use it when assessing 'A'. In Chapter 1, I emphasised that when I refer to 'A' I am referring to the aspect of the situation that the person was in that they were most disturbed about or found most problematic. This is often an inference which may be accurate or inaccurate, but I am not concerned about the realism of 'A' at this point. This is the reason why I prefer the term 'adversity' to the term 'activating event' which Ellis (e.g. 1994) used throughout most of his career[2] since it clearly indicates that 'A' is negative.

Identifying 'A' is not easy, and I have experimented with some techniques to help me do so over my career. I now use a technique that I have called 'Windy's Magic Question' (WMQ) because I have found it the most effective and efficient way of assessing 'A' of all the methods I have used. I describe its use in Table 2.1 with Saisha.

Assuming 'A' is true

Once the volunteer and I have jointly assessed the person's adversity (i.e. 'A') as featured in their target problem, it is important that

Table 2.1 **Windy's Magic Question (WMQ) with Saisha**

The purpose of this questioning technique is to help the volunteer to identify the 'A' in the ABC framework as quickly as possible (i.e. what the volunteer is most disturbed about) once 'C' has been assessed, and the 'situation' in which C has occurred has been identified and briefly described.

Step 1: I asked Saisha to focus on her disturbed emotional 'C' (here, 'anxiety').

Step 2: I then asked her to focus on the situation in which 'C' occurred (here 'being at a social gathering and talking to three people that I don't know').

Step 3: Next, I asked Saisha: "*Which ingredient could I give you to eliminate or significantly reduce 'C'?*" (here, anxiety). (In this case, Saisha said "the other people not judging me negatively if I say something stupid or boring".) At this point, I took care that Saisha did not change the situation (i.e. she did not say something like "talking to people I know with whom I feel comfortable").

Step 4: The opposite is probably 'A' (e.g. "the other people judging me negatively if I say something stupid or boring"), but I checked to see if this was the case. I asked: "*So when you are talking to the three people at the social gathering whom you did not know, were you most anxious about them judging you negatively if you say something stupid or boring?*". If not, I would use the question again until Saisha confirmed what she was most anxious about in the described situation.

I encourage the person to assume temporarily that 'A' is true. This is the case, even if 'A' is clearly distorted.

There are two main reasons for taking this approach with the volunteer. First, however unlikely it is that 'A' occurred or will occur, its occurrence is possible, and thus, it is important for me to help the person deal with it if it occurs. When a person is anxious, they predict the imminent presence of a threat. Discovering that the threat 'A' did not happen does not help them the next time they infer the imminent presence of the same threat. People who are anxious about failing are often precisely those who have not failed at anything.

Second, and perhaps most importantly, assuming that 'A' is accurate helps the volunteer and myself go on to assess 'B' (see later). If I helped the volunteer to correct the distortions in their 'A' without identifying and working with 'B', then they may well not experience disturbance at 'C', but this will not be because they have changed their rigid / extreme attitudes at 'B'. They would thus be vulnerable to such disturbance the next time they inferred the presence of 'A'.

Agreeing to deal with the adversity

Once 'A' has been assessed, and the volunteer has been encouraged to assume temporarily that it is true, then I will make sure that they are fully on board with this strategy and understand that the purpose of the conversation is now to help them to deal with the adversity that we have both identified. If they disagree, I will seek to understand their view and respond to any misconceptions that they may have of the approach that I am advocating. However, ultimately I will go along with the volunteer's view and help them as *they* best see fit[3].

Being goal-oriented with respect to adversity

I will assume that the volunteer has agreed to deal with the adversity in the remainder of our conversation. Given this, it is important to help them to set a realistic goal so that they deal with the adversity in healthy and constructive ways. This goal provides a forward-looking structure for the conversation. When I help the volunteer to set a goal with respect to their target problem, I again use REBT's ABC framework (see Chapter 1). As when assessing the person's problem, I may use this framework formally with the volunteer, but more often I use it to guide my interventions and will not necessarily refer to the goal-related ABC framework explicitly. Let me briefly provide a reminder of each of the elements of this framework when helping the person to set a goal:

'A' stands for 'adversity' which is the aspect of the situation that the person was most disturbed about in their target problem. As I have stressed, I see it that my main objective as an REBT therapist is to help the person deal constructively with the adversity that features in their problem. As such, 'A' is the same in both the volunteer's problem and their goal.

'B' stands for the flexible and / non-extreme basic attitude that the person holds towards the adversity and which largely accounts for their healthy response to the adversity.

'C' stands for the emotional, behavioural and cognitive consequences of the above basic attitude. Given that these reflect a desired healthy response to the adversity, then the person will tend to experience a healthy negative emotional response to the adversity[4], act constructively and subsequently have thoughts that are balanced, undistorted and non-ruminative.

There is no set point in the process when it is best to help the volunteer to set goals. However, it should be noted that if I ask a volunteer to set a goal at the outset, I would probably get a different response than if I ask about their goal once I have assessed the 'A' and 'C' components of their problem. It may also be wondered why I am dealing with goal-setting with respect to the target problem before I have finished my assessment of this problem. Thus, it should be noted that I have not yet assessed the 'B' component of their target problem. The reason will become apparent in due course, but, in short, I have developed a method[5] for assessing both the person's rigid / extreme attitudes and their alternative flexible / non-extreme attitudes towards the adversity at 'A' and then showing the volunteer the connections between their problematic responses at 'C' and the healthy alternative responses which should also serve as their goals, also at 'C'. Thus, I need to have established the volunteer's goals before I use this method.

The adversity in goal-setting remains the same as in the problem

As I mentioned earlier in this chapter, my goal as an REBT therapist in a VBTC is to help the volunteer deal healthily and effectively with the adversity that features in their nominated problem. As such, when helping the volunteer to set a problem-related goal, the adversity at 'A' in the goal-related ABC is the same as in the problem-related ABC.

Helping the volunteer to set goals at 'C'

When helping the volunteer to set goals, I begin by asking them to nominate emotional and behavioural goals and sometimes, if relevant, cognitive goals.

HELPING THE VOLUNTEER TO SET AN EMOTIONAL GOAL

As discussed in Chapter 1, REBT holds that when a person experiences a disturbed emotion about an adversity (known as an unhealthy negative emotion or UNE) it is healthy for them instead to experience an emotion that is negative in experiential tone but healthy in effect. This is known as a healthy negative emotion (HNE). I discussed the issue of UNEs and HNEs in depth in Chapter 1 and present each of the eight UNEs with their healthy HNE alternatives in Appendix 1. For convenience, I list these in Table 2.2[6].

Table 2.2 **Unhealthy negative emotions and their healthy alternatives**

Unhealthy Negative Emotion	Healthy Negative Emotion
Anxiety	Concern
Depression	Sadness
Guilt	Remorse
Shame	Disappointment
Hurt	Sorrow
Problematic Anger	Non-Problematic Anger
Problematic Jealousy	Non-Problematic Jealousy (or Relationship Concern)
Problematic Envy	Non-Problematic Envy

I may begin the emotional goal-setting process by asking the volunteer what would be for them a healthy emotional response to their nominated adversity at 'A'. If they respond by saying that they want to feel less of the disturbed emotion (e.g. less anxious), I will explain the problems associated with this goal as in the following dialogue (also see Chapter 1 for a discussion of this point).

Example. In this example with Saisha, I have just asked her what emotional goal she has with regard to dealing with the adversity of being judged negatively for saying something stupid in the specific situation of a social gathering. She replied – "to feel less anxious" – to which I responded as follows.

WINDY: OK, that is problematic, in my view. Would you like to know why I think that?

[This is a common question that I ask in VBTC. It preserves the active alliance between myself and the volunteer, and once they have agreed, then they become more open minded.]

SAISHA: Yes, please.
WINDY: Well, would you agree that anxiety is not helpful to you?
SAISHA: Definitely.
WINDY: It is a bit like cancer. If cancer is dangerous, can a small dose of the disease be helpful?
SAISHA: I guess not.
WINDY: So, if I could help you to have an emotion about people's possible negative judgment of you that would still be unpleasant to feel, since this would be a negative situation for you, but one that would help you to stay in the situation and participate in it[7] and one that would not involve you judging yourself negatively, would you be interested?

[What I have done here is to stress that such an emotion (i.e. an HNE) would still have a negative feeling tone, but would have constructive consequences.]

SAISHA: Most definitely.
WINDY: Great. I call that emotion 'unanxious concern.'
SAISHA: That makes sense.

HELPING THE VOLUNTEER TO SET BEHAVIOURAL GOALS

Helping the volunteer to set behavioural goals is often easier than helping them to set an emotional goal. I often find that I introduce such goals when outlining the behavioural associations of the HNE proposed as the emotional goal.

Example. When I asked Saisha about her behavioural goal, she referred to those associations (i.e. staying in the situation and speaking up):

WINDY: Rather than stay silent and looking to escape the situation, what would you like to do instead?
SAISHA: Well, as you just said, staying in the situation and participating in it would be good.

HELPING THE VOLUNTEER TO SET COGNITIVE GOALS

As I discussed in Chapter 1, cognitive consequences of rigid / extreme attitudes tend to be skewed to the negative, highly distorted and ruminative in nature. By contrast, cognitive consequences of flexible / non-extreme attitudes tend to be balanced, realistic and non-ruminative. When helping a volunteer to set cognitive goals, I take the cognitive consequences of their rigid / extreme attitudes and use the 'balanced, realistic and non-ruminative' criteria in encouraging them to do so. In my experience, unless the volunteer's cognitive consequences of their rigid / extreme attitudes are a central feature of their problem, I probably do not have time to set alternative cognitive goals within a VBTC context. However, when I do this, I take each of the person's highly distorted negative consequences, ask the person to develop realistic and balanced alternatives and invite them to set these as their cognitive goals.

Assessing 'B'

Having helped the volunteer to identify the 'A' and 'C' components of their target problem and to set healthy goals at 'C' in response to the same 'A', I am ready to help the person to identify 'B'. As with assessing 'A', I have experimented with different ways of assessing 'B' and having done so, I devised a method which, in my view, is one of the most effective and efficient ways of doing so. It is called 'Windy's Review Assessment Procedure' (WRAP) – see Table 2.3. In this table,

Table 2.3 **Windy's Review Assessment Procedure (WRAP) with Saisha**

Purpose: Once 'C' (e.g. 'anxiety') and 'A' (e.g. 'the other people judging me negatively if I say something stupid or boring') have been assessed, this technique can be used to identify both the person's rigid and alternative flexible attitude and to help them understand the two relevant B-C connections. This technique can also be used with any of the derivatives of the rigid and flexible attitude pairing. In the example below I worked with Saisha's rigid attitude and her alternative flexible attitude.

Step 1: I say: "*Let's review what we know and what we don't know so far*".

Step 2: I then say: "*We know four things. First, we know that you were anxious ('C'). Second, we know that you were anxious about the other people judging you negatively if you say something stupid or boring ('A'). Third, we know that your goal with respect to the problem is to feel concerned, but not anxious about such negative evaluation. Finally, we know that you would prefer them not to judge you negatively*".

Step 3: Now, I say: "*Now let's review what we don't know. This is where I need your help. We don't know which of two attitudes your anxiety is based on. So, when you are anxious about the people judging you negatively if you say something stupid or boring, is your anxiety based on Attitude 1: 'I would prefer them not to judge me negatively, and therefore they must not do so' ('Rigid attitude') or Attitude 2: 'I would prefer them not to judge me negatively, but sadly and regretfully, I don't have to get my preference met' ('Flexible attitude')?*"

Step 4: Saisha selected Attitude 1. If she was unsure, I would have helped her to understand this connection.

Step 5: Once Saisha was clear that her anxiety was based on her rigid attitude, I make and emphasise the rigid attitude-disturbed 'C' connection. Then I ask: "*Now let's suppose instead that you had a strong conviction in Attitude 2, how would you feel about the people judging you negatively if you say something stupid or boring if you strongly believe 'I would prefer them not to judge me negatively, but sadly and regretfully, I don't have to get my preference met'?*"

Step 6: If necessary, I would help Saisha to understand that this attitude would help her to achieve her goal of feeling un-anxious concern about the adversity. At this step, I make and emphasise the flexible attitude-healthy 'C' connection.

Step 7: I then ensure that Saisha clearly understood the differences between the two B-C connections.

Step 8: Finally, I helped Saisha to re-commit to un-anxious concern as her emotional goal in this situation and encouraged her to see that developing conviction in her flexible attitude is the best way of achieving this goal.

I show how I used this method to help Saisha to identify both her rigid attitude and alternative flexible attitude.

When using the WRAP method, I do the following:

- I show the volunteer that they have a preference which is common to both their rigid and flexible attitudes.
- I help the volunteer to see the relationship between their rigid attitude towards the adversity at 'A' and their disturbed responses to this 'A' (which is their 'C'). This is known as the problem-related 'B'-'C' connection.
- I help the volunteer to see the relationship between their alternative flexible attitude towards the adversity at 'A' and their healthy responses to this 'A' (which again is their 'C'). This is known as the goal-related 'B'-'C' connection.
- This method can also be used with any of the volunteer's extreme and non-extreme attitudes as well. If appropriate, I will help the person to identify their rigid attitude and the one extreme attitude that best explain their problem. I will also help them to identify the flexible attitude and the one non-extreme attitude that is related to their goal.

I do not carry out a case formulation, but I am guided by case formulation considerations

In cognitive behaviour therapy (CBT), it is common practice to initiate treatment after a case formulation has been done. Persons (2008: 1–2) describes the case formulation CBT as:

> a framework for providing cognitive-behavior therapy (CBT) that flexibly meets the unique needs of the patient at hand, guides the therapist's decision making, and is evidence-based … The therapist begins by collecting assessment data to obtain a diagnosis and develop an individualised formulation of the case. The therapist uses the formulation to aid the work of developing a treatment plan and obtaining the patient's consent to it.

Treatment is then initiated.

While case formulation is a good way to initiate therapy when it is known that treatment will be ongoing, there is just not the time to do this in a VBTC. That being said, I am guided by certain case formulation considerations while having a VBTC. These relate mainly to ways that the volunteer may unwittingly maintain their problem. Thus, I may ask one or two of the following case-formulation questions in my conversation with the volunteer and make use of their answers during the conversation[8]:

- How does the volunteer try to avoid the problem?
- How does the volunteer act to keep themself safe?
- How does the volunteer attempt to eliminate experience?
- How does the volunteer try to make themself feel better when experiencing the problem?
- What usage does the volunteer make of alcohol, food and drink and how does this relate to the problem?
- What is the volunteer's reaction to their target problem?
- Does the volunteer over-compensate for having the problem and if so, how?
- Does the volunteer see any advantages to having the problem and if so, what are they?
- How does the volunteer involve others in their target problem and what is the effect of this involvement?
- Will the volunteer lose anything by achieving their goal and if so, what will they lose?

Engaging the volunteer in a dialectical examination of their attitudes

At this point in the VBTC process, the volunteer 'should' hopefully understand the factors that underpin and maintain their problem and the factors that would promote the solution to this problem. In particular, the two B-C connections have been established, and the volunteer can see that the most important factors that they need to change in order to achieve their goals are the rigid / extreme attitudes that underpin the problem. They also see that their goals are underpinned by alternative flexible / non-extreme attitudes[9]. Once this stage been reached, then I can engage them in what I now call a dialectical examination of both sets of attitudes. This process has been typically called disputing. However, this is often taken to be an adversarial process, and I prefer the more consensual, if cumbersome, term, 'engaging the person in a dialectical examination of their attitudes'. I use the term 'dialectical' here because, as the Collins English Dictionary notes, it is used 'to describe situations, theories, and methods which depend on resolving opposing factors'. As I stressed in Chapter 1, both rigid and flexible attitudes are opposites to one another as are extreme and non-extreme attitudes. The resolution in REBT depends upon the person choosing one set of attitudes to operate on going forward. If I have done my work effectively, this ideally will be the person's flexible / non-extreme attitudes. This process involves the following steps.

Helping the volunteer to see that they have a choice of attitudes and to make that choice

It should be apparent to the volunteer by now that their attitudes towards the adversity that features in their target problem can be either rigid or flexible and / or extreme or non-extreme. When I do this, I tend to compare one attitude at a time and contrast their consequences, as shown in the following example with Saisha.

Example. This how I implemented this technique with Saisha:

WINDY: Now, you have a choice of which attitude to hold towards the situation where the people in question may judge you negatively if you say something stupid or boring. You can either choose to have the attitude which you currently hold which is, 'I would prefer them not to judge me negatively, and therefore they must not do so' or the alternative attitude which is, 'I would prefer them not to judge me negatively, but sadly and regretfully, I don't have to get my preference met'. Now, if you choose the first one, you will feel anxious about such judgment, stay silent and look to withdraw from the situation. However, if you choose the second one, then you will feel un-anxious concern about such judgment, and you will stay in the situation and speak up. Now, which of the two attitudes do you want to operate on?

SAISHA: It is an easy decision. I choose the second.

[This is the type of response I am looking for, and I tend to get when I have done my job properly. When the volunteer is hesitant, this may indicate that they harbour a doubt, reservation or objection to developing the flexible / non-extreme attitude and / or surrendering the rigid / extreme attitude which I will explore with them once disclosed (see later).]

Encouraging the volunteer to give reasons for their choice[10]

Once the volunteer has chosen the flexible attitude over the rigid attitude, it is important that I ask them to give reasons for their choice. Thus, I explain that since I want the person to be certain that they have made the right choice, I will ask them some questions that will enable them to reflect on their decision. The following is a range of such questions.

The empirical question

When I ask this question, I take the volunteer's rigid attitude and their flexible attitude[11] and ask them "which attitude is true and which is false?" Once the person says that their flexible attitude is true and their rigid attitude is false, I ask them to give reasons to support their choice.

The logical question

When I ask this question, I again take the volunteer's rigid attitude and their flexible attitude and ask them "which attitude makes logical sense and which one does not?" Again, once the person says that their flexible attitude makes logical sense and their rigid attitude does not, I ask them to give reasons to support their choice.

The pragmatic question

Again I take the volunteer's rigid attitude and their flexible attitude and ask them "which attitude leads to healthy consequences for you and which one leads to unhealthy consequences for you?" As before, once the person says that their flexible attitude yields healthy consequences and their rigid attitude yields unhealthy consequences, I ask them to give reasons to support their choice. This usually involves them referring to the consequences that we have already identified earlier in the conversation.

Using a variety of methods

The previous questions can be incorporated into a variety of methods designed to help people understand clearly the basis of their choice to go forward with their flexible and / or non-extreme attitudes.

The friend dispute

The purpose of the 'friend dispute' is to help the volunteer to see that they have a more tolerant and compassionate attitude towards a good friend than they have towards themself. From there, I can encourage the person to adopt this same tolerant and compassionate attitude toward themself. It is the REBT version of 'how to be your own best friend' and is best employed with self-devaluation issues. An example with Saisha follows. Here, I am working on the situation where she thinks that people in the social gathering may judge her negatively and if this were the case her attitude would be 'I am stupid and worthless':

WINDY: So you think that you are stupid and worthless if these people judge you negatively for saying something stupid. Right?

SAISHA: Yes.

WINDY: Let's stand back and examine that. What's the name of your best friend?

SAISHA: Maya.

WINDY: Now let's suppose that Maya came to you and told you that people had judged her negatively at a social gathering for saying something stupid. Would you say to her, "Well that proves that you are stupid and worthless"?

SAISHA: No, of course not.

WINDY: Why not?

SAISHA: Because she is my best friend.

WINDY: Would you think of her as a failure?

[This is an important step to include in case Saisha would think of her friend as stupid and worthless even though she would not actually say this.]

SAISHA: No.

WINDY: How would you think of her in the event of other people judging her negatively for saying something stupid?

SAISHA: Well, it would not change my view of her. Even if she did say something stupid, she'd still be the same, Maya.

WINDY: The same fallible Maya?

SAISHA: Of course.

WINDY: So, let me get this straight. Maya says something stupid, people there judge her negatively for it, and she is the same fallible Maya. Under the same circumstances, you are stupid and worthless.

SAISHA: I see what you are saying.

WINDY: Now how about being consistent? Either you begin to view yourself as fallible, or you start viewing Maya and other people as stupid and worthless if they say something stupid and others judge them negatively.

SAISHA: So you are encouraging me to accept myself as fallible, as I would other people?

WINDY: That's right.

Teach your children well

This is a different version of the previous method. Thus, if one of the volunteer's children told the person that they had said something stupid and two other people had judged them negatively and the child said to the volunteer that this proves that they were stupid and worthless, how would the volunteer respond? In using this method, I would once again help the volunteer construct arguments in favour of the non-extreme attitude of unconditional self-acceptance that they would wish to teach the child and then show them it would be best if they adopt that attitude towards themself in order to be authoritative in their teachings as well as for their own well-being.

Exploring the volunteer's doubts, reservations and objections (DROs) to adopting flexible and non-extreme attitudes for themself

What often happens when working on attitude change in VBTCs[12] with people is that they may have one or more doubts, reservations and objections (DROs) to adopting flexible / non-extreme attitudes or surrendering rigid / extreme attitudes. I both ask the person for their DROs and look for their presence as indicated in the person's non-verbal or para-verbal behaviour. I will show how I did this with Saisha but refer the reader to Dryden (2001) for a full discussion of such DROs.

WINDY: So, let's take your rigid attitude, 'I would prefer them not to judge me negatively, and therefore they must not do so' and your flexible attitude, 'I would prefer them not to judge me negatively, but sadly and regretfully, I don't have to get my preference met'. Do you have any doubts, reservations or objections to developing the first and giving up the second?

SAISHA: (hesitantly) No.

WINDY: You seem hesitant.

SAISHA: Well, I know it sounds silly, but in my mind, if I give up my rigid attitude then it makes it more likely that I will be judged negatively.

[People's DROs are either likely to be based on misunderstandings of the concepts of flexible / non-extreme attitudes or, as in Saisha's case, the perceived functional features of rigid / extreme attitudes. My response is to first normalise the DRO before examining it with the volunteer.]

WINDY: That's understandable. Many people think that in the beginning. However, let's stand back and examine it, shall we?

SAISHA: OK.

WINDY: So you think that if you give up the attitude, 'I would prefer them not to judge me negatively, and therefore they must not do so', it means that you are more likely to be judged negatively, is that right?

SAISHA: Well, when you say it out loud, it sounds ridiculous.

[This is a very common response. Sometimes, hearing the DRO expressed out loud either by themself or by the therapist is sufficient for the person to dispel it. However, it is useful for the volunteer to develop their own dispelling argument.]

WINDY: In what way?

SAISHA: Well, how can an attitude that is in my head influence others' behaviour?

WINDY: And what's the answer to your own question?

SAISHA: Obviously, it cannot.

WINDY: It may be worth having a written reminder of that if you find yourself having the same doubt in the future.

SAISHA: OK.

WINDY: Although, your private attitude may not influence others, the behaviour that stems from that attitude might. So, if you stayed silent and withdrew from the situation would that influence the others' judgments of you?

SAISHA: Yes it would, but as I now see taking this tack reinforces the problem rather than solves it. I need to confront adversity and deal with it rather than continually avoid it.

[While we have dealt with Saisha's initially stated doubt about surrendering her rigid attitude, I decided to raise a related doubt in case it was relevant. However, as Saisha makes clear, while the behaviour related to her rigid attitude makes negative judgment less likely, she needs to face and deal with such judgment rather than avoid it.]

Encouraging the volunteer to practise the new attitude and / or constructive behaviour in the session

At this point in the conversation, I look for an opportunity where the volunteer can practise their new flexible or non-extreme attitude and act in ways that support its development. I use three ways of doing this: a) role play; b) two-chair dialogue and c) imagery.

Role play

There are a number of ways in which I may employ role play in a VBTC to facilitate the volunteer's learning. Here are some of the most common:

• I play a person in the volunteer's life (e.g. a partner), and the volunteer client is themself communicating to the other person having first gotten into a healthy frame of mind which I have already helped them to develop.

- I play the volunteer, and the volunteer plays the other person in the above scenario. This can be used when the person has found being themself difficult in the role play. Having modelled healthy communication and the healthy attitude that underpins such behaviour, you switch roles, and the volunteer can be themself again.
- I play the rigid / extreme attitude part of the volunteer, and the volunteer speaks from their flexible / non-extreme attitude part of themself. The purpose of the resultant dialogue is for the volunteer to strengthen their conviction in their flexible / non-extreme attitude.
- I play the flexible / non-extreme attitude part of the volunteer, and the volunteer speaks from their rigid / extreme attitude part of themself. The purpose of the resultant dialogue is for me to demonstrate ways of responding to the rigid / extreme attitude to which the volunteer had struggled to respond when they spoke from their flexible / non-extreme attitude part of themself. Roles are then reversed to enable the volunteer to gain experience in responding effectively to their rigid / extreme attitude.

Two-chair dialogue

In two-chair dialogue, the volunteer switches between chairs in communicating with another person – the volunteer plays both parts – or with another part of themself. Again the ultimate purpose of such dialogue is for the volunteer to gain experience of acting constructively while rehearsing a flexible / non-extreme attitude. I recommend Kellogg's (2015) innovative work on transformational chair-work in this context.

Imagery

In using imagery, I encourage the volunteer client to imagine that they are facing in the present an adversity which features in their target problem and in doing so, they imagine themself holding the flexible / non-extreme attitude that I have helped them to develop and then acting constructively. Because, in most cases, when the volunteer faces the adversity, in reality, they will first respond by holding their original rigid / extreme attitude and then respond to this attitude with their flexible / non-extreme attitude, I suggest that the volunteer builds this process into their in-session imagery. Otherwise, they may get discouraged when they find that their first attitudinal response to the adversity in real life is a rigid / extreme one.

Encouraging the volunteer to get the change process underway as quickly as possible

The most important part of the VBTC process is one over which I, as therapist, have no control. This is where the volunteer chooses whether or not to implement what they have learned from the process in their life after the conversation has ended. If they choose to do so, I will not have the opportunity to review with them what they did. What I can do is to encourage the person to practise what they have learned in a relevant imminent situation, as soon as possible. Thus, I encouraged Saisha to talk to people she did not know at a social gathering two days after our VBTC and to rehearse her flexible attitude towards being judged if she said something stupid or boring while staying in the situation and speaking up. Where appropriate I suggest to the volunteer one or two of the following principles:

- Use a brief and memorable version of your flexible / non-extreme attitude.
- Make your behaviour consistent with the flexible / non-extreme attitude you wish to develop.
- Have your flexible / non-extreme attitude in your mind before acting on this attitude.
- Practise holding your flexible / non-extreme attitude and acting constructively while facing the adversity listed in your target problem.
- As you face your adversity, you may find yourself slipping back into holding your rigid / extreme attitude. This is normal and as such, respond to it with your flexible / non-extreme attitude when this happens.
- You will experience discomfort during this whole process of change. Expect this and tolerate it. Remind yourself that it is in your long-term interests to do.

- If necessary, rehearse what you plan to think and do in your mind's eye before you do so in real life.
- Recognise that you may be tempted to keep yourself safe while facing your adversity. It is best not to act on this urge. If you do so, you will not help yourself in the long-term.
- Commit yourself to regular practice of your flexible attitude and the behaviour that supports it.
- If you keep practising, your feelings will eventually change.
- Look for ways of generalising your learning from the adversity listed in your target problem to other adversities.

I do want to reiterate that I would want the volunteer to go away with only one or two of these points. If I encouraged them to remember them all, they would probably not remember any. On the other hand, as I will offer them the recording and transcript of the session (discussed later), they could reflect on such principles if I covered more than one or two.

Offering cod liver oil with the sweetener of adverbs and humour

When I grew up in the 1950s, it was common for young children to be given daily liquid cod liver oil for health reasons. It was something that I really did not look forward to because although my mother told me it was good for me, it smelt and tasted foul. I use what I call 'the cod liver oil moment' in a VBTC to alert the volunteer that they need to digest something unpleasant that is good for them in the longer term if they do so. In helping the person digest the unpleasant news, I some-times use adverbs which emphasise the unfortunate nature of the point to be digested. I also use humour to ease the 'digestion process'. In the presented VBTCs, I made eight references to what I call 'cod liver oil moment' [see Chapters 5 (three times), 6 (twice), 8, 9 and 11]. I had previously explained this concept to the group who attended my workshops from which the volunteers were drawn, so they would have understood the idea. Here is an example with Prats (see Chapter 11):

PRATS: I do not deserve it.
WINDY: No, OK. Let me ask you a question: are you ready for the cod liver oil?

PRATS: Yes.

WINDY: Are you ready?

PRATS: Yes.

WINDY: Are you sure?

PRATS: Yes.

WINDY: Here we go, let me ask you a question: you don't deserve it, right?

PRATS: Yeah.

WINDY: Why do you have to get what you deserve?

PRATS: Yeah, I don't.

Humour

I have referenced my use of humour specifically when discussing the cod liver oil moment, but I use humour more widely in VBTCs. Unfortunately, this does not come across well through the written word. So, what I have done is to show readers in the transcripts in Chapters 3–13 when I was using humour by making specific reference to such instances. Trust me, it is funnier on tape than in print!

Working with unique issues when the volunteer is a trainee REBT therapist[13]

As I have mentioned, all the volunteers whose conversations appear in Chapters 3–13 were participants in a workshop series that I conducted in Mumbai in November 2017. In this book, I regard them as trainee REBT therapists. When I work with such a group of volunteers, I face a number of unique issues.

A little knowledge is a dangerous thing

Trainee REBT therapists know more about REBT than other therapists and the general public. This can be a double-edged sword. On the positive 'edge', they are familiar and basically agree with the idea that responses to adversities are largely determined by attitude. On the negative edge, they may pay more attention to what they believe they should know about REBT than to the way they actually feel-think-act when discussing their problem with me. Sometimes, I encourage the volunteer to 'forget about REBT for the moment' when we are discussing their problem.

Neither allowing themselves to have strong preferences, nor strong negative, but healthy emotions

One of the most important, but least appreciated, aspects of REBT theory is that there is nothing wrong with having strong preferences. Indeed, they show us what is really, really important to us. Psychological disturbance occurs not when a person does not have one of their strong preferences met, but when their attitude towards this adversity is rigid. When the person's attitude towards the adversity is flexible, then the person's emotions will be strong in intensity, negative in tone, yet healthy in effect. Few REBT trainees grasp this point. They think that psychological health is associated with having weak desires and when these are not met, with having mild negative emotions. Thus, with several volunteers (e.g. with Megha in Chapter 7), I encourage them to acknowledge their very strong desires.

Difficulty in acknowledging problems and in admitting to holding rigid / extreme attitudes

People think that when they begin to train in REBT that a) they are not supposed to have problems and / or b) that their attitudes must only be flexible and non-extreme. Both of these are misconceptions and given a moment's reflection what these views indicate are that as soon as a person begins to train as an REBT therapist, their problems immediately disappear and their rigid and extreme attitudes miraculously become flexible and non-extreme. The likelihood that this will actually happen is very slight! If the person holds the first misconception, it is unlikely that they will volunteer for a VBTC and if they hold the second, they will voice flexible / non-extreme attitudes when they actually hold rigid / extreme attitudes. If I suspect that this is the case, I again encourage the volunteer to forget about their training to be an REBT therapist and just to think of themself as an ordinary human being struggling with a problem and to speak from their real, experiential self.

Problems in engaging with the dialectical examination of attitudes

It is sometimes difficult to engage a trainee REBT therapist in a dialectical examination of their attitudes because they know what the correct responses are to the key questions. In this case, I place more emphasis on them acting in ways that are consistent with their flexible and non-extreme attitudes, since this is where the most therapeutic value is to be had.

What will my peers think?

Let me reiterate that the VBTCs that appear in this book were done with volunteers from a group of people who were attending a worshop series on REBT. They were thus discussing their problems in front of their peers and sometimes a volunteer wants to show these peers how 'rational' they already are. One way that I try to minimise this is to seat the volunteer so that they can only see me and not the observing group. Another way is to encourage the group to focus on my interventions and try to figure out what I am doing as an REBT therapist. These two strategies are designed to encourage the volunteer to focus on me in the first case and to know that the audience is also focused on me and not them, in the second.

However, this need to be 'rational' is sometimes evident during our conversation. When the person can't focus on their problem because of it, I will deal with this issue in the 'here and now' where the inferred negative judgement from the watching group is the adversity at 'A' (e.g. "If I am not rational, my peers will think badly of me"). Once I have dealt with this, I help the person to concentrate on their target problem and proceed as before. If their target problem reflects the same theme (i.e. it involves dealing with negative judgement), I will focus the conversation on how the volunteer can generalise what they learned from dealing with the presumed negative judgement of the watching group to the adversity that features in their problem.

Key point. The key point in working with a volunteer who is a trainee REBT therapist and seeks help for a problem is to encourage them to bring themself to the conversation rather than the trainee REBT therapist. When this happens, the volunteer is likely to get more out of the VBTC then when it does not happen.

The use of the digital voice recording and transcript in VBTCs

One of the ways that I hone my VBTCs skills is by recording each interview with the permission of the volunteer and listen to the recording after a period has elapsed so I can then listen with a fresh self-supervisory perspective. However, the main purpose of making the recording is to send it to the volunteer soon after the VBTC has finished, if they write to me to request it. The reason why I invite them to request the recording is twofold. First, they may not want it, and thus, if I send it to them as a matter of course, it may be an unwarranted intrusion. Second, it communicates that I expect them to continue to take an active role after the VBTC has been concluded.

If they request the recording, I will also send them a written transcript of the session done by a professional transcriber. I have found that both the recording and the transcript aid the volunteer's reflection process after the conversation and serve to remind the person of what we discussed and what they learned. Sometimes, these materials enable the volunteer to focus on aspects of the process that seemed more important on review than they did at the time.

Different volunteers value the recording and transcript differently. Some value both, while others value one over the other, partly dependent on their learning style. Volunteers who relate more to the written word value the transcript, while others who learn better by listening will listen to the recording on an MP3 player, smartphone or tablet. Volunteers who do not like listening to the sound of their voice definitely prefer the transcript. It is for these reasons that I offer them both the recording and the transcript on request.

Summary

In this chapter, I have introduced the main ideas that guide my REBT practice in VBTCs. In particular, I have shown how I use REBT's ABC framework to do the following:

- Select the volunteer's target problem and work with a specific example of it
- Assess the target problem
- Set problem-related goals
- Deal with the rigid / extreme attitudes that lie at the base of the person's disturbed response to the adversity that largely features in the problem

- Develop alternative flexible / non-extreme attitudes that will help the person respond healthily to the same adversity and help the volunteer to commit to these attitudes
- Help the volunteer to identify and respond constructively to any doubts, reservations or objections that they may have to the above process
- Help the volunteer to practise these new attitudes in the session
- Encourage them to implement their learning as soon as possible in a relevant context.

Also, I discussed the unique issues that may occur when having VBTCS with volunteers who are trainee REBT therapists and the use of digital voice recordings and transcript in VBTCs.

In each of the next 11 chapters, I present and comment on a VBTC that I had with a volunteer during a series of workshops that I gave in Mumbai in November 2017. Each of the volunteers discussed a problem of daily living for which they genuinely sought help. At the end of each chapter, feedback is provided by the volunteer, seven months after the conversation took place (see Appendix 2). The feedback appears in the volunteer's own words.

Notes

1 Called 'quantum change' by Miller and C'de Baca (2001).
2 However, even Ellis (e.g. Ellis & Joffe Ellis, 2011) used 'adversity' to refer to 'A' in the latter part of his career.
3 I think that this shows that I practise therapy flexibly and not rigidly (Dryden, 2018b).
4 As the adversity at 'A' is negative, REBT theory stresses that it is constructive for the person to have an emotional response to the adversity that is negative and healthy.
5 I call this method 'Windy's Review Assessment Procedure' (WRAP).
6 See Appendix 1 for a comprehensive listing of the differences between UNEs and HNEs.
7 It is often helpful to use constructive behavioural associations here which are the functional opposite to the person's unconstructive behavioural responses to the adversity outlined in the person's problem-related ABC. As you will see, these serve as the person's behavioural goals.
8 It should be noted, however, that it is very unlikely that I will ask all of the following questions.

9   Given that all the volunteers in the book have been exposed to and are knowledgeable about REBT, reaching this stage should be straightforward.

10 A comprehensive discussion of the empirical, logical and pragmatic status of rigid / extreme and flexible / non-extreme attitudes is beyond the scope of this book. See Dryden (2016) for such a discussion.

11 The questions that follow can also be applied to the volunteer's main extreme and non-extreme attitude.

12 As well as in other forms of REBT.

13 By 'trainee REBT therapist' in this particular context, I am referring to people who were working therapeutically with people and were training to be REBT therapists or interested in undertaking this training.

Chapter 3

Family conflict

Overview

In this very brief therapeutic conversation lasting 17 minutes 43 seconds, Diya discusses a family conflict situation with her in-laws. Her in-laws do not get on with her parents and they do not talk to one another. Diya does talk to her in-laws, but she is anxious that they may say derogatory things about her parents to any child that she may have in the future. Her anxiety is based on the extreme basic attitude that if this happens it 'almost questions my existence'. I help Diya to see the connection between this attitude and her anxiety and help her to set concern as a goal if it happens rather than anxiety. Diya also wants to assert herself with her in-laws about them bad-mouthing her parents but her assertion is inhibited by her anxiety. The work that I do with Diya in this VBTC is centred on helping her to see that while her existence is based on things like air, food and water it is not based on her in-laws refraining from saying derogatory things about her parents. I help Diya to see that this new non-extreme attitude will help her to assert herself with her in-laws while recognising that while her wishes are important to her, her in-laws do not have to comply with them. With this in mind Diya resolves to discuss the matter with her in-laws.

The VBTC

WINDY: OK, Diya, what relationship problem[1] can I help you with today?

DIYA: So it's about me and my in-laws, and I got married in a very unconventional way, so to say, because, even though it was arranged by my parents and my in-laws, yet like how the whole arranged system has become more forward that, when the girl and the guy meet, then the parents are involved later on. My parents and my husband's parents didn't get along very well.

WINDY: With one another?

DIYA: Yeah. So, we called off the wedding at that point.

WINDY: Because of that?

DIYA: Because of that.

WINDY: So you got along with your husband-to-be.

DIYA: Yeah.

WINDY: But you could see that your respective parents didn't get on, so you called off the relationship.

DIYA: Yeah. And my parents had certain concerns and his parents had certain concerns. So me and my husband, at that point, couldn't deal with so much; there were too many things happening with them not getting along. But, yet, after a lot of time, we decided that, no, we wanted to get married to each other.

WINDY: So, you then said, because of the fact that you really wanted to get married, that overrode.

DIYA: Yeah, plus we spent more time with each other, so we got to know each other more and, what we thought in the beginning, like we like each other, that became stronger that we could override this hiccup of them not getting along.

WINDY: Why do you say 'hiccup' like that?

DIYA: Because here parents getting along with each other is part of the whole social structure.

WINDY: Sure.

DIYA: And, if they don't get along, it comes in the way of socially interacting.

WINDY: Yeah, it's an obstacle.

DIYA: It's an obstacle. And we tried to get both the parents involved, to get on with the plan. They didn't exactly get on with the plan.

WINDY: What was the plan?

DIYA: For me and my husband to get married and them being a part of that wedding.

WINDY: Right.

DIYA: Since they didn't want to be a part of that, me and my husband still went ahead and got married.

WINDY: Without either set of parents there?

DIYA: Yeah, without either set of parents.

WINDY: Without them knowing?

DIYA: Well, his parents knew, my parents didn't know.

WINDY: OK. I bet they were delighted (said with humour).

DIYA: Yeah, they were delighted, but they were not part of the small, we did a court marriage. So, his parents were not there for the wedding because their condition was, 'If her parents are there, we will not be.' It was this, then that. It has been three years now we've been married, and both the parents don't talk to each other. It's fine to the point that they are fine with me, they have a good relationship with me. My parents have a very good relationship with my husband. My anxiety starts, and, in fact, now it is even bothersome for me more that, since I know my in-laws and it is a relationship now that I have with them, but, if I am planning to have a kid, and if this still continues of, well, they don't like my parents, I am anxious in terms of that. I don't know what to do. I constantly have these thoughts, what if I displease them? What if they get angry? There are so many thoughts that I get, and I get worried about it and how am I going to balance this out, because they are very clear that, 'We don't want to talk to your parents.' But, along with that also, they are not even OK with a lot of their traits or their behaviour.

WINDY: Whose traits and whose behaviour?

DIYA: My parents, the way they are. My parents' traits or my parents' behaviour or my parents, the way they are.

WINDY: So, at the moment, you have actually got a system whereby you get on with your parents-in-law.

DIYA: Yeah.

WINDY: Your husband gets on with his parents-in-law, i.e. your parents, and the two sets of parents have agreed that they don't get on at all and, therefore, they're not going to see one another.

DIYA: Yeah.

WINDY: So why couldn't that continue indefinitely?

DIYA: Because … when there is a kid involved, there are going to be questions. As of now I don't mention …

WINDY: A kid involved, they see the grandchild separately.

DIYA: That is fine, still, but, when they start to say certain things, what bothers me is, when my in-laws would say certain …

WINDY: Like what?

DIYA: Derogatory things about my parents. Then it will bother me. It will bother me to the point that …

WINDY: So you're scared that your in-laws might say some negative things about your parents to you?

DIYA: And to my child as well.

WINDY: And to your child as well.

DIYA: Yeah.

WINDY: Yeah.

DIYA: To me, I can maybe, I don't know, ignore it or not rustle, but I would not like it if it goes to my child.

WINDY: 'Because, if they say negative things about my parents to my child,' what?

DIYA: ... That's almost questioning my existence.

WINDY: It questions your existence?

DIYA: Yeah, because I am a product of my parents.

WINDY: True.

DIYA: And ... that's going to be my child as well, so a part of me is with my child. So, constantly, I don't know how to process this.

WINDY: Yeah, if you're basing your existence on whether or not your parents-in-law say nice or nasty things to your child, you are bound to be anxious, aren't you? Now what's your goal?

[After giving Diya some time to talk and provide me with the relevant context, we focus on a major problem for her. Using REBT's ABC framework – see Chapter 1 – she is anxious (at 'C') about her parents-in-law saying nasty things to her child (at 'A'). Please note that Diya also provides her extreme attitude (at 'B') in her own words ('If they do, it questions my existence') without too much prompting from me. While volunteers sometimes disclose their rigid / extreme attitudes without much prompting from me as therapist, most often they don't. Once I have Diya's problem, I ask her for her goal which is a typical strategy in VBTCs.]

DIYA: ... That, irrespective of whatever they say or wouldn't say, I should be comfortable with having a child and with ... [pause] maybe standing up, also, sometimes to them; telling them that I don't like this.

WINDY: OK. That's a separate issue. Let's leave that for a minute.

DIYA: Yeah, but I'm not dealing with my anxiety.

WINDY: Yeah. So, instead of anxiety about your parents-in-law saying nasty things about your parents to your child, what do you think would be a healthy emotional response to that adversity?

[Initially, Diya says that she wants to feel comfortable irrespective of what her parents-in-law say to her child. However, this is not the

adversity and her stated goal is not sufficiently focused on her adversity.
So, I make my goal-question more specific.]

DIYA: ... [Pause] I don't know. I really don't know. I can do concern.
WINDY: Concern.
DIYA: Yeah ... but ...
WINDY: But what? You don't want to be concerned?
DIYA: No, I want to be concerned.
WINDY: Well, then I can help you to be concerned. What's your reservation?

[Don't forget that Diya is knowledgeable about REBT so she knows
that concern is the healthy alternative to anxiety, but she seems to be
doubtful about concern being her goal. So I enquire about this.]

DIYA: ... I don't know. What is my reservation?
WINDY (said with humour): If I knew that, I would be able to cure
    you without even knowing what you're saying, because I'd go
    into your mind, do a little bit of reorganisation, and that would
    be it. I'm afraid you're going to have to help me.

[This humorous intervention is partly intended to lighten the discussion
and partly to make a connection with the audience.]

DIYA: Yeah, I feel as if I've turned into this sort of control freak that
    I wish this never happens.
WINDY: I know, but let's just focus on the question of concern as a
    healthy alternative to anxiety. Leave the control-freakery to one
    side, OK? So, let's just focus on concern. What are your doubts
    and reservations and objections to feeling concerned about the
    prospect of your in-laws saying bad things about your parents
    to your forthcoming child? Do you have a child at the moment?

[I am unclear about whether the issue of being a control freak is a res-
ervation or a separate issue. I proceed as if it is a separate issue, but
I wish I had clarified this first with Diya.]

DIYA: No, but we are planning. That is my biggest anxiety, not to
    go ahead.

WINDY: OK, so what's your doubts, reservations and objections to concern, if you have any?

DIYA: ... No, there aren't. I mean I would be concerned. I don't know what action I will take if I'm concerned.

WINDY: Well, you mentioned it, which is assertion, didn't you?

[Here, I am making a link between assertion as a behavioural goal associated with concern and what Diya said earlier.]

DIYA: Yeah.

WINDY: Because, if you're anxious and you're questioning your existence, you're too busy asking yourself, 'Do I exist?' to assert yourself with your in-laws.

[In this intervention, I am showing Diya the B-C connection. If she questions her existence at B, it will inhibit her assertion at C.]

DIYA: Yeah, that makes sense. If I know what I'm going to do with my concern, which is I will assert myself, then I don't have it.

WINDY: OK. So you were saying earlier that your anxiety seems to be related to you questioning your existence, should your parents-in-law say bad things about your parents to your child.

DIYA: Yeah.

WINDY: Is that right?

DIYA: Yeah.

WINDY: Is that the root of your anxiety?

DIYA: Yeah, it is.

WINDY: So help me to see how your existence depends upon whether or not your parents-in-law say good or bad things about your parents to your child?

[In this intervention, I am helping Diya to question her extreme attitude.]

DIYA: ... [Pause] ... I don't know. If have to put it in words, the best way I can describe what happens to me is that I did go against them to get married.

WINDY: You did?

DIYA: Yeah.

WINDY: Yeah, you went against them.

DIYA: Against my parents, and I'm happy about that, but saying negative things about them doesn't really ... help.

WINDY: Doesn't help who?

DIYA: Doesn't help anybody.

WINDY: Well, that's true.

DIYA: It doesn't help me and it doesn't help them.

WINDY: That's why it's an adversity.

DIYA: Yeah.

WINDY: It's something bad. So, we know that them doing that is unhelpful all round; it's an adversity.

DIYA: And maybe I can deal with, if they would do that with me, but my child, why I'm concerned is because I feel it's unnecessary to do that.

WINDY (said with humour): It is unnecessary, but people have been doing unnecessary things since God invented Adam and Eve. It was unnecessary, right from the start, for them to eat the apple.

DIYA: Maybe what is important to me, now that I am thinking, when I am talking about it, why I question my existence is somewhere I feel like my child should also see my parents in a good light and in a good way, and, hence if they would talk negatively, maybe my child will then think negatively about me as well. These are the two lines of thoughts.

WINDY: What would your child call your parents-in-law when they're old enough?

DIYA: The Indian version?

WINDY: Yeah.

DIYA: They would call them Dada and Dadi.

WINDY: OK. This is the logic: 'Dada and Dadi think badly of.'

DIYA: Nana and Nani.

WINDY: OK. So the child's logic is this: 'Dada and Dadi think badly of Nana and Nani, therefore, since mummy comes from Nana and Nani, I don't think nicely of mummy.' Is that how it goes?

DIYA: No, I don't think that will happen.

WINDY: That's what you're saying.

DIYA: Yeah.

WINDY: Right? Incidentally, if your child does think like that, are you saying that there's nothing that you can do to say to your child something like, 'Well, you know, that's Dada and Dadi, that's what they do, they think badly of Nana and Nani. Oh well, they're fallible human beings who are doing wrong'? Why can't you train your child to be rational about their irrational grandparents?

DIYA: So I think that way, but then there are days when I feel like what if I get super angry with my in-laws?

WINDY (said with humour): If you get super angry with your in-laws, you use super REBT on your anger.

DIYA: Yeah.

WINDY: Because you are rightly saying, 'I don't want my parents-in-law to say nasty things about my parents to my child,' right? Fantastic, even if we put a few 'verys' in there. But your super anger, isn't your super anger coming from, 'And, therefore, they absolutely must not do so'? Now why aren't they allowed to do the wrong thing?

[Here, I help Diya to connect her anger about her parents-in-law's behaviour and her rigid attitude about it.]

DIYA: Yeah, of course they're allowed to do.

WINDY: Why can't you see that you can still exist whether or not they say these bad things about your parents?

DIYA: … [Pause] … Yeah.

WINDY: You see, you're probably correct at some point that your existence depended upon your parents, because, if your parents didn't feed you, change you and things like that, you would've died. But aren't you saying something similar like, 'Right now, forget about them feeding me, but I have to be fed good things only about my parents otherwise my existence goes' (said with humour)? What do you think of that idea, when you stand back and look at it?

[Here, I show Diya that her existence probably did depend on her parents when she was very young, but her existence does not depend upon her parents-in-law saying good things about her parents to her future child.]

DIYA: … [Pause] … No, it's not dependent.

WINDY: I'm sorry, I'm deaf. I'm 67, I can't hear.

[Here I humorously invite Diya to repeat this more loudly to help increase her level of conviction in her flexible attitude.]

DIYA: My existence can't only depend on being fed good things about my parents.

WINDY: What is your existence dependent on?

DIYA: Basic things like breathing and eating.

WINDY: That's right. So, if you say, 'I'm going to exist until I don't exist because I can't get enough water, air. I would like them to say good things, or perhaps even not to say bad things', because I don't think you're saying that you want them to say good things.

DIYA: Yeah.

WINDY: You're saying you don't want them to say bad things.

DIYA: Yeah.

WINDY: So that's the main thing. 'But I'm not bringing that into my existence. I can exist even though they think that way or say those things, but I don't like them and I really wish they wouldn't do it, and I'm going to assert myself every time they say that.' Right?

DIYA: Yeah.

WINDY: Now why couldn't you develop a plan based on 1) showing that you could counter any negativity that your parents-in-law give your child – you see the child more than they would see them – and you can help them to be rational about that when the child's old enough; and 2) that your existence doesn't depend on whether they say bad things about them – you can exist until you don't exist through lack of air – but you would prefer them not to say these things, but that doesn't mean that they must not do so. Now, if you did all that and then asserted yourself, and, if you asserted yourself, what would you say to them?

DIYA: That, 'I would like you to not say negative things to my child, because that would influence him or her negatively, and … I would appreciate it if you don't do that.'

WINDY: And I would add, 'You don't have to do what I want, but, since this is important to me,' and if your husband backs you up on that – will he back you up on that?

[Here I encourage Diya to voice her new flexible attitude as part of her assertive message to her parents-in-law.]

DIYA: Yeah.

WINDY: OK, you do it together, right, that's probably the best thing to do, but to show them that they don't have to do it, but, because you would appreciate it, and then say, 'Can we agree that you don't do that?'

DIYA: Yeah.

WINDY: And then you shake them by the hand. I don't know what the Indian equivalent of a gentleman's handshake is, but you do that. So that's the treatment plan that you can do. Now what do you think of that treatment plan?

[Diya commits herself to assert herself with her parents-in-law concerning them not saying bad things about her parents and reiterates that they do not have to do what she prefers them to do.]

DIYA: That's a good one.

WINDY: Do you think you'd be able to do it?

DIYA: Yeah, I'll be able to do it.

WINDY: Let's see if you do.

Follow-up: seven months later[2]

I had presented with anxiety to Dr Dryden. Anxiety related to me having a child. It was linked to other people's behaviour. What I learnt was my need to control my tendency to conclude or link their behaviour to me. The problem was resolved to a large extent because even though I had presented it only in this area since that's an event that I am focussing on right now, but this underlying thought has been with me for years. I stopped feeling the pressure rising from the anxiety and the thought of controlling the outcome.

Dr Dryden helped me to identify this in just a matter of a few minutes. And he didn't say what is wrong with me but the way he questioned or directed me, helped me to myself identify my inherent automatic thought pattern. By identifying this thought pattern I could break out of it. He directed me in a manner which felt as if I could easily and naturally correct or change that thought, not making it sound as if it is impossible or difficult to stop feeling the anxiety. In fact, his style of session felt as if it was simple to make the change in my thinking and behaviour.

As a practitioner of REBT, I learnt the ease with which one can make the client realise his own inner thought pattern. And help them with behavioural change without aggressively telling them what to do. So not only I learnt how to apply it to myself but also with my clients.

After my session with Dr Dryden, it felt easy and possible for me to change and behave differently. I thank Dr Dryden for helping me and teaching me so much which I can and will use in many areas of my life.

Notes

1 The workshop that Diya is attending is on REBT and relationship problems.
2 See Appendix 2 for the letter I sent to volunteers requesting a follow-up.

Chapter 4

Loss

Overview

In this VBTC lasting 20 minutes 43 seconds, Em T presents with what she refers to as procrastination. After much exploration, I discover that after getting married and living in close proximity with her in-laws, she feels that she had lost the freedom, autonomy and joyousness that she had when she was single and living with her parents. While happy with her husband she is struggling, in particular, with her mother-in-law's impatience. What she sees as her own rebelliousness is an attempt to stay connected with her past life rather than grapple with the adversities involved in her new life. I help Em T to see that she can feel sad about the loss of her previous life and accept her mother-in-law as someone who will listen to her but who needs periodic reminders to do so. I encourage her to acknowledge that while she no longer has the unfettered autonomy of her previous life with her parents, she does have more limited autonomy in her present life, but that she is not exercising it. I suggest that buying a light covering of her own choice can be a symbol of her autonomy and that through acceptance of her mother-in-law and by exercising what autonomy she does have in her current situation, she can eventually rediscover her old joyous self.

The VBTC

WINDY: OK, Em T, what problem can I help you with this evening?

EM T: Since the last one year, I noticed a big difference in the kind of person I am. Until last year, I have always been extremely proactive, all deadlines met, anything that had to be done, whether

WINDY: How long have you been married for?

EM T: Ten months.

WINDY: Ten months ago. OK, so let me summarise. Before you got married, you were a joyful, proactive doer.

EM T: Yes.

WINDY: Then you got married and you turned into a rebellious, non-joyful, not doer. Now I wonder what could explain that? It beats me (said with humour). Can you help me understand that a little bit more?

[The change in Em T can be traced to getting married, but we don't know, as yet, what the adversity was and is.]

EM T: So, if it's anything to do with my husband and me, I will do it happily, but for myself or for my family, I don't want to do anything.

WINDY: So, you've experienced a fundamental shift in yourself, haven't you?

EM T: Yes.

WINDY: OK. And do you see yourself as a wife?

EM T: Slowly, yes.

WINDY: So, are you saying that you would still happily do things for your husband?

EM T: Yes.

WINDY: Out of love or duty?

EM T: No, love.

WINDY: OK, so you love your husband and you would happily do things for him, but something's changed in you since you got married.

EM T: Yes.

WINDY: Have you got any idea what that might be?

EM T: I don't know.

WINDY: Think about it.

EM T: ... Like I mentioned earlier, I think I'm overworked also, but I cut down on my work.

WINDY: But that doesn't explain the fundamental shift.

EM T: It took me a while to transition into accepting the new family as my family. It's funny, I felt it was wrong to call someone else mum and dad. So, all of that took me a while, but now that's not an issue. So, I don't know ...

WINDY: So, in this new house that's still only got bulbs, who lives there?

I wanted it or someone else wanted it, I've done it, on time, maybe before time. But, since about eight to ten months, I feel that I just keep procrastinating; I don't wish to do things. I know I'm overworked, but I feel, whenever I do have the time, I just still tell myself, 'I'm tired,' or, 'I don't want to do that.' When someone else, in fact, tells me, I rebel by not doing it. I don't identify with that person anymore, so I also feel guilty about that.

WINDY: So, up to ten months ago, you were a person who would hand in work on time, even early, for yourself and for others?

EMT: Yeah.

WINDY: Then that changed – I want to go into that with you. Now you've become a person who kind of rebels against people who want you to do certain things, even against yourself.

EMT: Even against myself.

WINDY: And it's interesting that you use the word 'rebellion', because it feels that it's a part of you that is rebelling?

EMT: Yes. At times, yes.

WINDY: And, as a result of that, you feel guilty about what?

EMT: I don't know. That's not my value. We spoke about values. The values I set for myself would be to do things; I would do them happily. Now there's not so much joy in doing them; it's tedious.

WINDY: And so, you're going against your value which is to do things joyfully.

EMT: Yes.

WINDY: So, you're not doing things unjoyfully, it sounds like, and you feel guilty about the lack of joy?

EMT: Yeah, lack of joy or … yeah, I guess. I mean I was more social, I would be more proactive and maybe organise things, do things. Now I just don't do it, and I feel that I'm moving away from people and from myself maybe.

WINDY: OK, let's cut to the chase. What happened ten months ago for this to change?

EMT: So, the biggest change in my life ten months ago was that I got married, but I don't know. We moved into a new house and we moved in July, and, until now, we just have bulbs; I have not put lights. So, I've been procrastinating to just go and purchase lights, to get curtains. I just can't get myself.

WINDY: So, before you moved, where were you living?

EMT: With my parents.

WINDY: And your husband, or you got married?

EMT: No. So, we got married.

EM T: Just my husband and me, and my in-laws are just right opposite our house. So, it's the same corridor, just across.

WINDY: Is that relevant at all?

EM T: Yes, because we spend most of the time together and we just come to sleep in this house, my husband and I.

WINDY: So, you spend …?

EM T: Most time together, with the whole family.

WINDY: OK, and you're happily doing that or not?

EM T: Not really. I used to be a very talkative person. Now I don't like to talk too much. I don't like to interact.

WINDY: So, what is it about this new role you've got as part of this? It sounds like you're part of that family now.

EM T: Yes.

WINDY: And you can't be yourself in that family, can you?

EM T: No, I can. When you asked me that question, I just realised something. A lot of times I think, at least in India, or at least I was brought up in a way where sometimes you're told, when you get married, you're supposed to take on certain responsibilities. At my parents' place I could just chill and maybe order around, which I never did.

WINDY: Order around?

EM T: Yeah, just tell my mum or someone. We had domestic help so, 'Can you just get me this?' I never did that, but I knew I had the luxury.

WINDY: You could do it if you wanted to.

EM T: I could.

WINDY: But you didn't.

EM T: Also, I have the luxury, I do it, but somewhere I know that more things are expected out of me, and I think the rebellion comes from that; that I don't want to do it; why should I?

WINDY: OK. So, let's have a look at the situation. So, in actually getting married and living with this new family, you have the option of help but you don't use it, but you've got expectations that are on you which you don't want.

EM T: Sort of.

WINDY: What kinds of expectations are we talking about?

EM T: Like … if there are guests, then you need to be on your toes, serving people all the time. The same things I used to do very happily earlier, but now I don't know, I don't like to do it.

WINDY: Because?

EM T: ... I don't know. I just feel like I want my space. I don't want anyone to tell me anything.

WINDY: OK, so it sounds like what I was talking about, like an autonomy issue – you've lost autonomy, haven't you?

[My role at this point is to help myself and also Em T to understand her behaviour and to what aspect of her new status as a wife who lives in very close proximity to her in-laws she is responding. We slowly hit on lack of autonomy as the adversity she has a problem with at 'A'.]

EM T: I think so, yeah.

WINDY: Yeah, because your autonomy was that, 'Look, I could lounge around if I wanted to, I had a choice, but I didn't. Now I haven't got the choice. I've lost that autonomy, and I'm going to rebel against it.' So, who else knows how you feel in your family? Does your husband know how you feel?

EM T: My husband knows.

WINDY: About the loss of autonomy? Have you told him that?

EM T: Not in these exact words.

WINDY: No. What have you said to him?

EM T: I've told him that I don't like to be told, and, when I'm told, I somehow don't do it. And I have the thing that they don't really communicate, my in-laws, that I should be doing.

WINDY: They don't communicate?

EM T: About certain things, like what I'm thinking, like, 'You should be doing this because you are the daughter-in-law.'

WINDY: They don't say that?

EM T: They don't say that. So, my mum-in-law's nature is very different from mine. I get things done but she is impatient, so she'll keep repeating things, 'This has to be done, this has to be done.'

WINDY: To you?

EM T: To me.

WINDY: And what do you say to her?

EM T: I will be like, 'Yeah, relax, we'll get it done, we'll get it done,' and the getting done, I have now reached a point where I won't do it.

WINDY: 'You can't tell me what to do.'

EM T: Yeah, like, 'Stop telling me.' It's not like, 'You can't tell me,' it's, 'Stop telling me.'

WINDY: Well, that's what I meant, 'Stop telling me what to do.'

EM T: Yeah. I know it has to be done and nobody had to tell me twice to do something.

WINDY: So how do you feel about her putting things on you?

EMT: ... I mean the only word I can think of is stressed. I feel pressure.

WINDY: I'm hearing anger.

EM T: ... [Pause] Yeah, I feel a little bit. I don't know if it's anger. I can't really do it right now.

[Em T did not resonate to feeling angry, so I dropped the issue.]

WINDY: OK. What would you like to say to her, ... if she was open?

EM T: She is. So, I have communicated to her that we function differently, and I'm someone who gets things done, and, because of the lack of time, I can't do certain things, so let's take it easy.

WINDY: Yeah, but she doesn't listen.

EM T: No, she will listen for a month, and then she'll be like, 'OK, OK, this has to be done.'

WINDY: OK, yeah, and what do you make of that then? Why do you think she does that?

EM T: Because, for her, she still finds joy in little things and she wants to do it.

WINDY: OK, so the question is how can you allow her to be her, because she's going to do it? It's like a user manual: you say, 'No, I don't like this,' and she puts the user manual down and she makes a great effort for a month, and then afterwards she forgets and she picks up the user manual and she goes back to it, and you may have to say, 'Remember?' So how can you allow her to be her, and maybe remind her of what you want, while retaining autonomy yourself?

[The 'user manual' concept that I introduce here is one that I discussed during the workshop in which Em T was a participant. The point is that everybody functions and responds in different ways and that we lack a user manual to understand how that person 'works' so that we can get the most out of our relationship with them.

I then help Em T to see that she needs to accept her mother-in-law as she is, to remind her periodically of her own preferences while retaining her own sense of autonomy.]

EM T: ... [Pause] I don't know. ... [Pause] I often pass it off humorously, and I do certain things which I know have to be done, so, to maintain a balance, where I am even communicating that it can irritate me at times and let's get a balance.

WINDY: OK. So, let me put this to you: what conditions would have to exist for you to reconnect with your joyful, proactive self? If I had a magic wand and could change the conditions, and you'd go back to being the joyful, proactive you, what would those conditions be?

[Here I ask Em T a variant of what I have called 'Windy's Magic Question' (see Chapter 2) in order to identify more clearly her adversity at 'A'.]

EM T: ... I don't know.
WINDY: Tell me.
EM T: ... Live with my parents.
WINDY: Live with your parents, yeah, so you can go back to being what?
EM T: ... [Pause] I don't know. I don't know what.
WINDY: So you miss being there, don't you? It's like being homesick in a way.
EM T: ... And the funny thing is I don't stay far away, but I don't live with them.

[Em T is quite upset at this point.]

WINDY: No, and so living with them, that's the fundamental shift, isn't it? You've gone from living there ...
EM T: To visiting.
WINDY: Yeah. And so, what would happen – and I'm not suggesting it, but I'm just playing around with some ideas – if you and your husband went to live with your parents? I'm just playing around with ideas now, assessing things. What would happen?

[At this point, I am not clear about the adversity so, I am taking what Em T has discussed and, as I say, I am playing around with some ideas to get a more accurate assessment of the important factors in Em T's problem.]

EM T: ... I don't know.
WINDY: Is that allowable in your culture?
EM T: No.
WINDY: OK, it's not allowable, but it's still something that you want.

EMT: ... Yeah.

WINDY: Your tears are telling me what you want. So, your desire, and it's a strong desire because it's backed up with emotion, is, 'I really, really, really, really want to go back and live with my parents.' Now is that something that has to be or doesn't have to be?

EMT: It doesn't have to be, but I would like it.

WINDY: But you'd really like it. Therefore, there's going to be a sadness because you've experienced a loss and you've experienced a transition, and you're moving into a new situation, and you've been rebelling against it. I'm not sure that you've really understood why. So, what does this realization now mean to you that, 'Look, I really, really miss being with my parents and I really miss the me that I was when I was there.' But it doesn't have to be that way because it can't be that way. Now the question is, 'How can I acknowledge that loss, acknowledge that sadness and go and grab the joyful and proactive me that's still stuck there?' it seems to be, isn't it? 'So how can I go get that girl and bring her into my life, but without losing that sadness, that loss?' Now how can you do that?

EMT: Accepting that I got married because I wanted to.

WINDY: Yeah. And whose choice was that?

EMT: Mine.

WINDY: Sorry?

EMT: Mine.

WINDY: Look, I'm an old man. You've got to shout.

[As I did with Diya in Chapter 3, I encourage Em T to make a more definite statement of healthy thinking, in this case a statement of her own autonomy.]

EMT: It's mine.

WINDY: OK, so you've exercised autonomy, but you didn't quite recognise, at the time, what it would mean, did you, and how you would feel? You'd thought you would go from being joyful, proactive there, to joyful, proactive there, and you're not. But now you realise what's happening, you still have autonomy; it's a different kind of autonomy. What are your choices?

EMT: What are my choices?

WINDY: Yeah.

EMT: As in I didn't get it.

WINDY: What are your choices now?

EM T: To go back to being myself or to just ruin it.

WINDY: OK, so what one thing would give you a sense that you're going back to yourself? If you could imagine one thing that you would do or that would say, 'Hey, that reminds me of someone,' what would it be?

EM T: Getting anything done.

WINDY: OK, name me one thing that needs to be done.

EM T: The light bulbs.

WINDY: OK, so Professor Dryden shares light on the subject, at last … *[Em T and members of the audience laugh at this pun]* … So, what would you have to remind yourself, rather than to see this as a chore, to see this as actually an expression of autonomy, joy and proactivity?

EM T: That I think this would be more than I did for me to get to live with my husband in a house of our own, and do it up the way I want.

WINDY: Right. So this is a statement of the fact, 'I want this and this is a house of our own, even though we've got some aspects that I don't like.' Again, I think with your mother-in-law, she's like a Duracell battery that needs replacing after every month, and the replacement is the reminder. You may have to remind her, and she may never get it in the sense that you don't have to stop reminding, but what would happen if you reminded her once a month, when she reverted? What do you think would happen?

EM T: She'll listen and she'll work on it.

WINDY: Right, and it's only going to last a month.

EM T: But it'll make me feel motivated to work on myself as well together.

WINDY: Exactly. OK, 'So every month I'm going to have a word with my mother-in-law and change the battery if I need to, but, in the meantime, I'm going to shed some light and make this house joyous' (said with humour), because I think part of it is, I talked about how the environment is actually expressive of how you feel, these lights are an expression of, 'no, no, I want to go back there because that's where I'm joyous.' But you can be joyous there as well, if you really accept the fact that you do feel sad and you have lost something important to you, but that you haven't lost autonomy, and that your real proactivity and joyfulness is not frozen and stuck there. You were happy there but you could create, if you chose to, a different thing. Change the light bulbs with that in mind, and not just the light bulbs.

[I am aware at this point that I am doing much of the work here. But I am thinking that Em T will soon have a recording of the VBTC and a typed transcript so that she can process the points more fully. In the final part of the session, I bring together a number of important points:

1. *Em T needs to realise that she has lost something important when she got married. She lost the freedom and autonomy to do things in her own way. It is important that she acknowledges this loss and feels sad about it.*
2. *She can accept her mother-in-law as a person who will listen to her, but needs monthly reminders so that she will continue to do so.*
3. *What she called her procrastination can be seen as a form of protest to maintain her autonomy.*
4. *Em T can live within the constraints of her current situation, but still realise that she has autonomy which she can assert. Thus, she can choose the form of light covering even if she buys it at the shop recommended by her mother-in-law.*
5. *In realising and acting on these points she can rediscover her proactive, joyous self.]*

EM T: Yes.
WINDY: This change of light bulb is a change in you.
EM T: Yes.
WINDY: Will you do that?
EM T: Yes, I will.
WINDY: When are you going to do it?
EM T: I have to go to a specific store that she's told me, so that's going to be next weekend.
WINDY: Has she told you which specific light covering to get?
EM T: No.
WINDY: So that's your autonomy. You've got the reality of the order, but the freedom of choice within that. So you choose exactly what you want.
EM T: Yes.
WINDY: When do you think that's going to happen?
EM T: Next weekend.

WINDY: OK, so I think you should take a picture for me and send it to my website. I want to see a before and after. Will you agree to do that?

EMT: Yes, I will.

WINDY: I want a picture of it now and a picture of it then, and a reminder of how you made that change.

[Em T did not contact me with these pictures.]

Follow-up: seven months later[1]

It has been a year since I saw a drastic change in myself and it led to severe internal conflict as I couldn't identify with the person I had transformed into. I did have awareness in the root cause of the problem but what struck the most with me was the ease with which Professor Dryden hit the nail on the head and tied it to 'loss' – loss of autonomy. It struck a chord with me, and he helped me to accept the undesirable change in myself which I abhorred, with more compassion. At an emotional level, I feel alleviated from the pain and way more accepting and forgiving towards my own self as against getting angry.

I helped another friend who went through a similar phase make sense out of her distress. I am grateful to him for helping me out!

Note

1   See Appendix 2 for the email I sent to volunteers requesting a follow-up.

Chapter 5

Lack of influence and involvement

Overview

In this VBTC lasting 17 minutes 36 seconds, Maia discusses two areas of her life where she lacks the influence that she demands that she has. In the first area, for reasons of care and love she wants her younger sister to follow a particular life script and is struggling because she holds a rigid attitude that this script must be followed. In the second area, Maia demands that she be involved in her sister's wedding despite the fact that her sister's future husband's family is traditional and does not involve women in the wedding plans. Maia holds onto these rigid attitudes strongly and I have to work in a very focused way to help her to loosen her grip on them using a lot of humour to make my questioning more palatable.

The VBTC

WINDY: OK, Maia, what problem can I help you with today?

MAIA: I've been finding myself extremely irritated these days, which I think is coming up from the anxiety that I have that my sister's getting married in two months. It's a love marriage, but the way it's been going on for the past couple of months, it's been going on as if it's an arranged marriage, which is something, I guess, the first thing that I'm not able to accept. Mine was a love marriage and we had done a register marriage, so the whole tradition, rituals, everything was not there. It was very simple. With my sister, what's happening is their caste religion is very close to ours, but still I find that a little more patriarchal than ours, and I think that that's what I'm not able to accept.

WINDY: Let me get this clear. What is patriarchal?

MAIA: The male is given a lot of importance, the male's family.

WINDY: In the family that your sister is marrying into.

MAIA: Yes. So, the boy is considered extremely important, the boy's family is directing the whole thing.

WINDY: It's more traditional.

MAIA: Yes.

WINDY: And your marriage was more?

MAIA: Mine was just a register marriage, so it was very simple, friends, very fun.

WINDY: Was that OK with you or would you have preferred a more traditional?

MAIA: No, I was OK with that.

WINDY: You were OK with that.

MAIA: It was my choice.

WINDY: It was your choice.

MAIA: And my husband's choice.

WINDY: OK, so his family is less patriarchal, less traditional.

MAIA: Yes. And the thing is she is voicing out her opinions in front of us that, 'Oh, they have said this,' but then she has her own way of doing. She wants to do certain things, but, in the end, she would end up agreeing to what they want.

WINDY: Right.

MAIA: So what is happening right now is that one thing is I'm a little anxious or scared that, once she goes there, I hope she's able to adjust well. She's going to move to Sydney.

WINDY: Can I ask you a personal question?

MAIA: Yes.

WINDY: How old are you?

MAIA: I'm 32.

WINDY: And she?

MAIA: She's two years younger than me.

WINDY: OK. And what's the dynamic in your relationship?

[I asked this general question because I wanted to understand the context for her emotional problem. Novice REBT therapists might be too focused on the specifics of the problem to do this.]

MAIA: We're very close, but I still kind of consider, because she's younger than me, as a kid.

WINDY: You regard her as what?

MAIA: As a kid, like my younger sister.

WINDY: I didn't quite hear that. When you get to my age you're a bit hard of hearing. Could you say it a little bit louder (said with humour)?

MAIA: As a kid.

WINDY: As a kid, OK. So, this is your kid sister.

MAIA: Yeah.

WINDY: And what do you want to do for your kid sister?

MAIA: I, somewhere, feel that I have to equip her to go there and live comfortably, have her individuality, and, if, God forbid, something goes wrong, she should be able to contact me and tell me. But I think I'm coming in ...

WINDY: That's an interesting script, isn't it? You write the script down: 'OK, this is how I'd like you to live your life.'

MAIA: Yes.

WINDY (said with humour): 'And this is what I want you to do. By the way, I don't come from a traditional family, nobody told me what to do, but that doesn't matter. I've got to protect you. Here's the script.' You could do all that. What's her choice?

[From an REBT perspective there is nothing wrong per se in Maia having a script for her younger as this is really a collection of preferences for how she would like her sister to live her life. The issue is whether her attitude is rigid (e.g. "I want my sister to live her life according to my script for her and therefore she has to do so") or flexible (e.g. "I want my sister to live her life according to my script for her, but she does not have to do so").]

MAIA: My choice?

WINDY: Her choice.

MAIA: Her choice is going on with it ...

WINDY: Or?

MAIA: ... whatever's coming through.

WINDY: Yeah, to go along with your script or to go against it, right?

MAIA: Yeah, to go against it.

WINDY: Does she have that option?

MAIA: Yes, of course, because she has her own script that she'll be following, so I should be allowing her to do that.

WINDY: We'll come along to that in a minute, that should, but let's take one should at a time. This is like rickshaws – they're all coming at once. So, one should at a time (said with humour). I think what you're doing, and the question is you do have an idea of how you'd like your sister to live her life, because out of love and care.

MAIA: Yes.

WINDY: Not because of control. Out of love and care. The question is does she have to follow that or not?

[Here, I validate Maia's preference before questioning the rigid component.]

MAIA: No, she doesn't, but it'd be nice if she does.

WINDY: I agree.

MAIA: Yes. So that she's safe and she doesn't lose her individuality.

WINDY: No, that's what I'm saying, you're doing this out of care, but do you recognise that she doesn't have to follow your script for her?

[Here I continue to validate Maia's preference before again questioning her tendency to make this preference rigid. I do this to strengthen the alliance before asking her to take a little dose of cod liver oil.]

MAIA: True, she doesn't have to.

WINDY (said with humour): Would you like a little dose of the cod liver oil now?

MAIA: Yeah, I guess.

WINDY: Because that's a difficult thing. You're opening up to the possibility that she may lose her individuality, and there's nothing that you can do. After you give her the script, are you going to go over to Sydney and live with them?

MAIA: And I hope she lives well, even if it is as for her script.

WINDY: Yeah, OK. But whose choice is it, whose script that she lives by?

MAIA: ... Hers, but I think hers is not as strong, so I feel like doing some rectifications there.

WINDY: That's fine. Do all the modifications or rectifications that you want, but does she have to go along with them?

MAIA: No.

WINDY: No, that's the thing. So, if you keep that in mind, and I think you need to keep the 'but' very clearly in mind: 'I'm doing this out of care and I think, because her script is not strong enough, I've got an opportunity to get in and tweak it a little bit, but, sadly and regretfully, she still doesn't have to accept my modifications.'

MAIA: Yes.

WINDY: Does she?

MAIA: No, she doesn't.

WINDY: OK.

MAIA: She doesn't have to.

WINDY: But it will be sad and annoying. What was that other 'should' that we talked about?

MAIA: The other should is related to the same thing, is I don't have a father and, when my father was there, I was considered a boy and doing everything in the house, which I am right now considering her marriage is coming up, so, in everything, anything and everything I'm involved, but it is this particular aspect in talking to that family that I'm not involved, and this is because I'm the girl.

WINDY: Yeah.

MAIA: If I was a boy, her older brother, I'm very sure I would've been there in the conversations, and I think that's where the irritation is coming from.

WINDY (said with humour): What about if you were transsexual?

MAIA: Then it would've been my mum's choice. I would've left it to my mother's choice.

WINDY: No, if you were part boy and part girl.

MAIA: Yeah, exactly, so it would've been my mother's choice, whatever she would have chosen whether to include me or not, I would've been fine. But I think right now I'm taking it personally, this one thing, is because of the fact that I'm not a boy, and that's why, for everything else …

WINDY: Well, you're not a boy, but you're used to being the role of the boy, aren't you?

MAIA: Yeah.

WINDY: That's what you're saying.

MAIA: Yes, and even right now.

WINDY: And, because you've taken the role of the boy and been used to taking the role of the boy, and want to be consulted, therefore what?

MAIA: Therefore I should be consulted and I should be included in the conversation.

WINDY: What kind of 'should' are we talking about?

MAIA: Even with the in-laws ...

WINDY: What type of 'should' are we talking about? Ideally, prefer-ably or absolutely?

MAIA: ... Because I practice REBT, I should say 'preferably'.

[This is an interesting point and one that is particularly relevant to this book. Trainee and novice REBT therapists, because they know the theory of REBT, tend not to admit to holding rigid attitudes towards adversities, even when they do. as was the case with Maia.]

WINDY (said with humour): Yes, you should, but I'm not talking to the REBT practitioner.

MAIA: Yeah, then I should be. Whatever happens, I should be in the conversation.

WINDY: That sounds like an absolute 'should'.

MAIA: Yes, absolute 'should'.

WINDY: OK, we know then that you have a strong preference about this.

MAIA: Very strong.

WINDY: It's really important to you, right, for all kinds of reasons – you're used to being consulted, you want involvement because you care about your sister, right, and that's fine. But does it have to be that way or doesn't it have to be that way, ultimately?

MAIA: It has to be that way.

WINDY: Well then how are we going to persuade God to make it that way?

MAIA: So I think I should go ahead and put up an example; but, even if I'm not consulted, I should put maybe my foot down and say, 'See, I need my voice to be heard.'

WINDY (said with humour): As long as you then put your head down first before your foot down and get your head around the idea that, 'It still doesn't have to be the way I want it to be,' and you're reluctant to do that.

MAIA: I am.

WINDY (said with humour): As a novice REBT practitioner.

MAIA: Well, I think, if it was someone else, I think it would have been simpler, but it is with me that I'm doing this.

WINDY: Special rules apply, we know that. Your clients' preferences don't have to exist, but, because it's you ...

MAIA: Because it's me.

WINDY: Yeah, and you occupy the unique role as a girl, but brought up as a boy, and people should understand and take that into account and give you a place on the table, right?

MAIA: Yes.

WINDY: That's what they have to do, right?

MAIA: Yes.

WINDY: Why do they have to do that?

MAIA: Because the change should come from us.

WINDY: OK, now I'll ask you a question again and I'll do an Albert Ellis on you, right?

MAIA: OK.

WINDY: Just because it's so important to you and you're used to it, why does it have to be that way?

MAIA: Because ...

WINDY: Wrong!

MAIA: Because ...

WINDY: Wrong!

MAIA: It shouldn't be.

WINDY: What was that?

MAIA: It shouldn't be.

WINDY: Yeah, because any 'because' you give is a reason for why it's desirable.

[What I call 'doing an Albert Ellis' here is using an approach used by Ellis with people who hold to rigid attitudes very tenaciously. He would ask for evidence in support of these attitudes and interrupt them immediately to show that any reason given is in support of the people's flexible attitudes. The only 'correct' answer to such questions is 'There is no evidence'. I do this with a lot of humour, mimicking Ellis affectionately as I do so.]

MAIA: Yes.

WINDY: And you're saying, 'Because it's desirable, that's the way it has to be. My desires, my unique desires have to be met.'

MAIA: True.

WINDY: Yeah. But do they?

MAIA: I should do that.

WINDY: What?

MAIA: I prefer not to put forward my desires so strongly when life doesn't have to always accept it.

WINDY: No, no, no, no, no. Put your strong desires forward as force-fully as you want, because maybe that's the way of getting their attention.

MAIA: Maybe that's where I'm going, like this bull-headed.

WINDY: No, no, no. You see, there's a difference between expressing your strong desires and demanding that they be met, and expressing your strong desires and not demanding that they be met.

MAIA: … OK, putting it forward and not demanding that they be met.

WINDY: But put it forward strongly if they are strong, OK?

MAIA: Yes.

WINDY (said with humour): But, you see, if you don't get that clear, you'll go into the situation and you'll go back to, 'Because they're strong, because it's my sister, because I've been used to it, because, because, because, therefore they have to,' and they don't.

[While a person may grasp the unrealistic nature of rigid attitudes in general, they may think that there are special reasons why their par-ticular rigid attitude is realistic. It is the REBT therapist's task to dis-abuse them of this often strongly held conviction.]

MAIA: Yeah.

WINDY (said with humour): Otherwise they'll be saying, 'Well, we don't usually include women, but strange forces are at work here. Maybe it's the 'must'. We didn't realise there was a 'must'. We don't have any power of choice.'

MAIA: True.

WINDY: Would you like another sip[1] (said with humour)? That's diffi-cult to digest, you know. So, if you really recognise that you care about your sister and you'd like to protect her, but she doesn't have to, because she may be your kid sister but she's how old?

MAIA: She's 30.

WINDY: So your 30-year-old kid sister. She'll always be your kid sister. You're 98, she's 96, she's still your kid sister (said with humour). I understand that. But she still has choices and she still doesn't have to do what you want her to do. For these people, yes, it would be nice if they include you, and, because they're trad-itional, they're not going to, so you need to be a little bit more present and forceful and express your strong desires, but watch your tendency is to transform your desires into rigid attitudes.

MAIA: Yes.

WINDY: Keep your attitudes flexible, but express your strong desires. Now do you think you can do that?

MAIA: I think there's a possibility now I can do that.

WINDY: OK, but be prepared for them to say, 'No, no, no, no, because you're a girl.' And then, 'I may be a girl, but I'm also a boy, because that's my tradition,' and so you can be forceful.

MAIA: Yes.

WINDY: But, in the final analysis, who's in charge of the decision-making there, the final analysis?

MAIA: ... I consider we, as a family. In this particular thing?

WINDY: Yeah, their marriage.

MAIA: Yeah, we, as a family, all three of us: my mother, myself and my sister.

WINDY: I thought the boy's family was.

MAIA: Yeah, but the thing is my mother's going, 'Yes, OK, yes, OK,' so they're just going on saying whatever they want, and we are just going on with, 'Yes, OK.'

WINDY: Right, so maybe you need to have a word with your mother as well, maybe to back you up.

MAIA: Yeah, which is why they say I'm becoming extremely rebel-lious; I'm becoming very angry these days and very anxious.

WINDY: Because?

MAIA: Because I'm voicing out my opinions, and they're scared, which I kind of agree too, depending on what I'm saying.

WINDY: Well, it depends, but, if you make a point of saying, and I do recommend this, 'Look, this is what I strongly want. You don't have to do it, but this is what I strongly want.' You express the idea that they don't have to do what you want, but you also express your preferences and the reasons for your preferences.

[Again, the REBT perspective on assertion is that when a person voices their desires in an assertive way to the other it is important that they make it explicit that the other doesn't have to meet these desires although the person wants them to do so. Making this clear to the other reminds the other that they have the freedom to comply or not and also reminds the person themselves of the flexible attitude on which their request rests.]

MAIA: Yes.

WINDY: And maybe they pick up on the idea that you may be sneaking in a little demand there.

MAIA: Yes.

WINDY: And that's what they're reacting to.

MAIA: Yes, they are.

WINDY: OK. So that's the way to keep your attitudes flexible and even, and to express your strong desires, OK?

MAIA: OK.

WINDY: So why don't you summarise what we've done today? What are you going to take away?

MAIA: My sister has her own script, she does not have to follow mine, even though I would prefer she does. As long as she's happy following her own script that's fine.

WINDY: Or even if she's not happy.

MAIA: Oh yeah, even if she's not happy. Yeah, I should be able to accept that. And, with regards to my second 'should' and demand, I would put forward my opinions, my thoughts, but I will not demand for it to be followed in the same manner.

WINDY: But you are going to put a case which reflects your strong preferences.

MAIA: Yes, my strong preferences strongly.

WINDY: OK, I think we've got time for one last gulp of cod liver oil. Are you ready for the last gulp of it?

MAIA: One more.

WINDY: OK, here's a scenario for you: your sister goes to Sydney and she's unhappy, and there's nothing that you can do to affect that. How do you feel?

MAIA: Extremely helpless.

WINDY: Yeah. You need to work on that, not here, but your emotional reaction means that's a real big issue. I'm not going to go into that with you, but I wanted to highlight that because it seems like that is a real issue for you. In the meantime, let's stick to the 'now', because she may go to Sydney and be perfectly happy after all.

MAIA: Yeah.

WINDY: But you need to deal with that somewhere along the line, should it happen.

MAIA: Yes.

[I was in two minds to raise this issue. On the one hand, I considered that it was something that Maia would struggle with and needs to give

some thought to how she could deal healthily with this adversity if it occurs. However, on the other hand, I was concerned about overloading her. I decided to raise it because she had the option of requesting the recording and transcript after the session which would remind her of the two main issues we dealt with and the third prospective issue.]

Follow-up: seven months later[2]

I enjoyed my session with Prof. Dryden. This session was a strong reminder for me that my loved ones have choices just like I do. I can certainly express my strong desires, in their best interest, but I need to remember not to allow them to transform into demands from them.

Honestly, there were a few moments when I found it difficult to apply any of the learnings attained during the session. But, I kept going back to the transcripts and recordings of the session to remind me what I forget – avoid making my strong desires to rigid attitudes.

Even today, I get the same anxiety-provoking thoughts. I feel helpless. But going back to the learnings from the sessions I had with Prof. Dryden, helps me get back to the moment. The jovial manner in which he struck the chords of simple common sense, has helped me to apply my learnings to my daily problems easily, whether it's my family, friends or colleagues.

In the end, he left me with a very bitter dose of cod liver oil – the possibility of something I dreaded. I have looked into it deeper and dealt with it by applying the same learning from the session. I believe I am in a much better state to face my fears now. I would really like to thank Prof. Windy Dryden for all the help he provided in the little time we had.

Notes

1   Of cod liver oil.
2   See Appendix 2 for the email I sent to volunteers requesting a follow-up.

Chapter 6

Anxiety about protecting son

Overview

In this VBTC lasting 14 minutes 51 seconds, Whisky discusses her
anxiety that her son may not reach his goal, which is to get into the
Army, because he is not doing all the things that he needs to do to
achieve it. She recognises that she does have a protective function as a
mother, but she has a rigid attitude towards discharging this function.
The result is that she and her son have developed an unhealthy relationship where she nags him and he does not listen to her. During
our conversation, I help her to see that she can flexibly discharge
her maternal responsibility, but that she can't make her son do what
she considers to be the right thing. Rather, she can encourage him
to take responsibility for his decisions. I put to her that in the final
analysis life may be more successful than her in teaching him the
consequences of his actions. We then discuss what she can say to her
son to indicate that while she has preferences for his behaviour, she
is no longer going to insist that he follows this path. If she does this
and she stops nagging her son this will probably lead to them having
an improved relationship which both seem to want.

The VBTC

WINDY: OK, Whisky, what relationship problem[1] can I help you
    with today?
WHISKY: It's about the relationship with my son.
WINDY: OK.
WHISKY: He is a 16-year-old raging teenager, and, for the last six
    months to one year, ever since he did his O-levels, he did pretty

well in his exams, and he has always been very unconventional as in not wanting to take instructions, not wanting to be told what to do. But, up until he was doing his last term, that was kind of acceptable and the pressure wasn't so much on, but now he's got certain goals in life. The way he carries on his day-to-day activities and his time management, we, as parents, or rather me more, do not see that being in sync with where he wants to be.

WINDY: Where does he want to be?

WHISKY: He wants to join the armed forces.

WINDY: Are you OK with that?

WHISKY: We are absolutely fine with that. We encourage him to do that, because that's what's going to make him happy, and we are happy with the decision. But there are certain ways of conducting yourself, if you want to reach there eventually, in two years. One is all about discipline and time management and fitness and incorporating academics in a reasonable proportion.

WINDY: And he has to show all these things to them before he gets in?

WHISKY: Well, it's a process. It's a part of the qualifying examination where he has to do reasonably well in his board exams, then the entrance exams and then qualify for the medicals. So it's a set of three steps.

WINDY: Wait a minute, so I can understand the fitness thing they're going to assess. How are they going to assess his time management?

WHISKY: Well, it's part of the discipline.

WINDY: Yeah, but how are they going to assess that?

WHISKY: They may not be able to assess that at the time of the exam, per se, but it will eventually reflect upon how well he can carry on with his activities, if he is so ill-disciplined.

WINDY: When he's in the Army?

WHISKY: Well, as he is now. The bone of contention is he just won't listen to us, and that's what it's all stemming from. And we tell him, 'It's your goal, it's your dream, and, if you want to reach that, there are certain things that you must do for yourself right now.' It's kind of coming to the relationship becoming worse. It's not just about, 'I won't do what you want,' but it's about, 'Don't nag me. Don't tell me. I know what's to be done.' It's kind of distancing himself.

WINDY: Yeah, and how do you feel about the fact that your son isn't listening to you?

WHISKY: It really, really upsets me. I'm very disappointed.

WINDY: What's upsetting to you that a 16-year-old son does not listen to his mother? Is that rare in India?

WHISKY: No, it's very common. I mean they suddenly change when they are in the middle of their teens.

WINDY: Right. So you're finding it very upsetting. What's upsetting for you about him not listening to you?

WHISKY: ... Primarily, the disrespect.

WINDY: So you see it as a sign of disrespect.

WHISKY: Yes.

WINDY: So it's not possible for him to respect you and not listen to you?

[Asking her this question helped her to identify her adversity a little later.]

WHISKY: ... [Pause] No, it's maybe not disrespect. It's about I can see disaster.

WINDY: You want to protect him.

[Here, I validate her preference to strengthen the working alliance and ensure that she knows that I understand her.]

WHISKY: Yes, I want him not to go down that line, and, as a parent, I feel a moral responsibility. He keeps going wayward and I want to keep bringing him into line, and that's where there is conflict.

WINDY: So, let me be clear, because I think, by questioning the disrespect, you may have got rid of it. If you really think about it honestly, are you upset because you find his behaviour disrespectful to you or because, in a way, that you're not able to exercise your protective function? What are you most upset about?

WHISKY: I'm not able to exercise my protective function.

WINDY: OK.

[Although Whisky initially said that she was most disturbed about her son's disrespect, it turns out that she is most disturbed about her not being able to exercise her protective function as a mother.]

WHISKY: I mean I could possibly even tolerate disrespect.

WINDY: As long as he didn't get into trouble.

WHISKY: Yes. I don't want him ending up disillusioned with life after two years, because time has gone and he can't get back to what he wants.

WINDY: At what point do you think he is responsible for himself and his own decisions?

WHISKY: ... Most of the way he conducts himself is ... he can think for himself, so I would think he's being very selective in not being responsible. He wants to make certain decisions and he says, 'I'm responsible,' whereas, when it comes to handling his own life and his academics and his career, he's not showing any responsibility.

WINDY: OK. Obviously, I didn't ask the question clearly enough. At what age is he responsible for his own decisions?

WHISKY: ... There are two different aspects to this: if it is legally or if it is making a decision and being able to say, 'Look, I'm an adult and I can take this decision,' that's 18.

WINDY: OK.

WHISKY: But, until then, it's a very grey area. You can always say, 'I'm grown up enough,' but how much is enough? Sometimes parents have a different version.

WINDY: OK. So. what's your goal in talking to me about this?

WHISKY: I want to be able to give up feeling so distressed about him.

WINDY: And feel what instead?

WHISKY: ... [Pause] I don't know. Feel ... as a parent I can't totally absolve responsibility, but maybe just let go.

WINDY: And what feeling would go with you letting go?

WHISKY: Maybe allowing him to make the mistakes and be OK with it.

WINDY: And what feeling would go along with that?

WHISKY: ... Trusting that he will eventually see my point of view, if I don't keep nagging him.

WINDY: That would be an outcome, but you see what we're talking about, what you're most concerned about is your failure to protect him from harm.

WHISKY: That's right.

WINDY: At the moment you're very upset about that prospect. So what I'm asking you is what would be a healthier emotion that would, in a sense, still allow you to do the best you can, but without the emotion. It sounds like this is something that you need to think about a lot.

WHISKY: I do think about it because it's happening every day.

WINDY: Yeah, so obviously you're preoccupied with it. Is your being preoccupied helping you?

WHISKY: I am able to make the disconnect once I'm in my work. I won't allow it to get in.

WINDY: OK, because you're distracted.

WHISKY: Yes.

WINDY: But how about at home?

WHISKY: It's there.

WINDY: OK, so how about I helped you to have an emotion that still treated this as something that you really don't want to happen and is an adversity, but that you would do the best you can and then, in a way, even when you're at home, to think about other things? How would that be?

WHISKY: … I tried, and it works sometimes and it doesn't.

WINDY: You tried what?

WHISKY: I tried keeping myself occupied with other things.

WINDY: No, I'm talking about the emotion. You see, at the moment what you try is based on disturbance; you're disturbed about this. You're concerned and disturbed. So I can help you to be concerned without the disturbance.

WHISKY: Yes, I think I would like to do that, yes.

[As can be seen I have to work quite hard to keep Whisky focused on a possible goal in the face of her adversity – failing to exercise her protective function as a mother. It is only when I distinguish between being concerned with disturbance and being concerned without disturbance that Whisky engages with the goal question and chooses the latter as her adversity-related goal.]

WINDY: So, OK, let's review what we know and what we don't know. We know that it's very important to you, as a mother, as a caring mother, to do your best to protect him from harm, right?

WHISKY: That's right.

WINDY: Now do you think you're doing that?

WHISKY: Yes.

WINDY: OK, fine. So, do you have to succeed or not?

[This is a very shortened form of Windy's Review Assessment Procedure (WRAP) which is designed to help the person to identify

*their rigid and extreme attitude to an adversity. I assume that her atti-
tude is rigid and question it. I would only do this with a person knowledgeable about REBT and even then, looking back, I wished I used a
fuller version of WRAP and then questioned her rigid attitude.]*

WHISKY: Not necessarily.
WINDY: OK, but you can still try without succeeding.

*[It would have been better to ask this as a question and not make it as
a statement.]*

WHISKY: Yes, of course.
WINDY: OK, so that's the important thing you need to remember,
that, 'I really want to try,' and you can write down the things
that you've tried that doesn't work. Nagging doesn't work.

*[I suggest a problem-solving method so she can collect data concerning
what works with her son and what doesn't. She can best do this when she
holds a flexible attitude and is concerned, not anxious, about protecting
her son, a point I make in the following.]*

WHISKY: No, it doesn't.
WINDY: OK. Often people think, 'Wait a minute, he's not listening
enough. Maybe he's like Professor Dryden, hard of hearing.
Maybe I'll talk to him again about it.' No, he's told you clearly
it doesn't work. So, once you are healthily concerned, but not
unduly anxious and upset about this, you might be able to engage
in that kind of problem-solving activity – what's the best way to
get through to him. But now this is the cod liver oil moment: let's
suppose that you do your best, and he doesn't listen and he continues in his undisciplined ways, and he doesn't get into the Army,
although the Army will soon shape him up, once he gets in there.
If he says, 'Don't nag me,' to his commanding officer, he'll be out
on his ear, so he's not going to do that. 'Don't nag me. I want
to stay in bed.' 'Out!' (said with humour). So, let's suppose the
worst, that he doesn't listen to you and he doesn't get into the
Army; he doesn't get what he wants. How do you feel about that?

*[What I call a 'cod liver oil moment' is helping a person to face an
adversity and to deal with it even though it's painful.]*

WHISKY: I'd be very disappointed for him.

WINDY: Right, but – and this is maybe the point – how would you view him? Would you view him as a poor person who's not getting what he wants or would you view him as a non-poor person who's not getting what he wants?

[Here I want us both to understand whether Whisky would be sad, but not depressed, for her son or would feel depression based on other pity for him. The former recognises that he is in a poor situation, but is not a poor person for being in that poor situation, while the latter involves her considering her son to be both in a poor situation and a poor person for being in that situation.]

WHISKY: I'd view him as a non-poor person.

WINDY: Good, because otherwise you would feel other-pity. So, you could say, 'Yeah, it's disappointing that he doesn't get what he wants.' Now what do you think he'll learn from that?

WHISKY: … If he doesn't get through?

WINDY: Yeah. What do you think he'll learn from that?

[Here I shift the focus away from Whisky to her son to help her consider that he needs to learn the consequences of his action and to take responsibility for them.]

WHISKY: … [Long pause] He probably will regret that he could've done …

WINDY: And what will he do?

WHISKY: … He would work for something in a better way towards something.

WINDY: OK, so now I've got another cod liver oil moment. Are you ready for it?

WHISKY: Yes, I am.

WINDY: Sometimes life is a better teacher than a mother. What do you think of that?

[I put it in this form because it is short and, hopefully, memorable. It is clear that at present Whisky's son is not listening to her and my point is that if he continues in this way he may not get into the Army, and if so, then life would have taught him the lesson that he may not get what he wants if he does not work for it.]

WHISKY: Yes, I agree with you.

WINDY: All you can do is what's in your control, but, if you let go of the idea that, 'I have to succeed,' and show yourself that, 'It wouldn't be terrible, and later on he'll learn the lesson, and, unfortunately, I can't make him do that, because, the more I make him do that, the more he's going to rebel against me.'

WHISKY: In the process, it's just accepting our relationship and what little time we have with us. It's not so nice.

WINDY: Yeah, that's right. He's not enjoying being with you when you nag him.

WHISKY: True.

WINDY: What are you a doctor of?

WHISKY: I'm actually a gynaecologist with infertility as my specialist, but I like working with mental health of women.

WINDY: OK, fine. So you could give birth to a new relationship with your son.

[This is typical of my work in that I try to use something in an unrelated area of the person's life to help them with their problem.]

WHISKY: I would love to know how I could do that.

WINDY: Well, first of all, step number one, stop nagging. Go up to him and say, 'You know, Son, although you're not 18, I'm going to stop nagging you. I've learnt, you've told me a great lesson, and I'm going to stop nagging you, because I enjoy your company. I know you don't enjoy mine when I nag you, so I'm stopping all that. And you know what, Son? I'm going to allow you to have the consequences of your decision, and, if you don't get into the Army, I'll feel very sad for you about that, but I think you might learn something about that. And you have an opportunity now, but that's up to you. So that's the last thing I'm going to say to you on the matter, so let's go out and have some fun.'

WHISKY: …

WINDY: Right?

WHISKY: It sounds like a good idea.

WINDY: Yeah? What would stop you from doing it?

WHISKY: … [Pause] Nothing. It won't stop me. I think I'll try doing that. It's just that I haven't been so open about it.

WINDY: Right, OK, and, if you're open about it, open to yourself and with him, and say, 'Look, I'm sorry, Son, I've been doing the wrong thing. I actually recognise that. I'm doing it out of love, but it's not working for you, so I'll stop doing it, because I love you and I want to hang out with you.' It means that you're going to have to take the consequences of your own decision, 'And I'm backing away from that. Anything I can do to help you, come to me and I'll be there for you, but otherwise I'm not nagging you anymore.' Do you think he'd like to hear that?

WHISKY: Yes.

WINDY: He probably wants to hang out with you, but at the moment you're stuck in a cycle, because you believe that you have to discharge your responsibilities by getting him to do the right thing. That's nice but it doesn't have to be that way.

[After giving Whisky some pointers about how to have a better relationship with her son, I remind her that if she holds on to her rigid attitude about discharging her maternal responsibilities then she will be stuck in the unproductive relationship with her son, which neither of them wants. However, I end on a positive note by reiterating the flexible position that she could take.]

Follow-up: seven months later[2]

I would like to describe my experience regarding the interview as unique and one of a kind. I personally have never had a chance to undergo such a self-introspecting conversation with anyone, wherein I was the one having to talk about or share my thoughts.

I found Professor Dryden very attentive, paying attention to minor details and very empathetic. This approach encouraged me to relax and be able to talk more and more freely about my most secretive thoughts. Despite there being a time limit, I did not feel rushed or hurried. Adequate attention was paid to my feelings and my responses. Professor Dryden's body language was one of deep involvement.

As for the actual problem, one session is way too less to have it solved. We all carry a lot of emotional baggage and to be able to offload it in just one session is not a joke. But yes, the session was definitely in the right direction.

After the session I was able to, in my own space and time, reflect upon what exactly happened and felt better equipped to deal with the situation, even knowing that such a session with him wouldn't happen

*again. There was no right or wrong. It was about each person's own
views and perspectives. There was no blame game.*

*Now after many months since the session I am a little bit more sorted,
though I reiterate the fact that just one session is not enough to even
figure out whether it was useful or if it had any deep, long-lasting effect.*

*The only drawback of the session I felt was that we had an audience
and somewhere it was a little difficult to be very upfront and share and
bare it all.*

*Overall it was a very enriching experience, and I am privileged to
have been a part of it.*

Notes

1   The workshop that Whisky is attending is on REBT and relationship
    problems.
2   See Appendix 2 for the email I sent to volunteers requesting a follow-up.

Chapter 7

Decision-making about giving birth

Overview

Megha's VBTC lasts for 21 minutes 27 seconds. She wants help with a decision that she has to make concerning where to give birth to her first child. As the conversation unfolds, it becomes clear that it is centrally important to Megha to have a natural childbirth, but she was reluctant to tell her husband how important it was to her because doing so means, in her mind, that she is being demanding and unfair to her husband. While I question these inferences, I encouraged her to tell her husband what she really wants and to invite him to work with her on this point.

The VBTC

WINDY: OK, Megha, what problem can I help you with this afternoon?

MEGHA: So ... I have been struggling to make a choice in terms of a place that I want to birth my child. I've been struggling quite a bit, going back and forth with a lot of doctors, and I'm very confused about the choice to make.

WINDY: So, what are the options?

MEGHA: So, the options are there are two doctors. Basically, I'm very, very somewhere staunchly towards wanting a natural birth, and, usually, in India the rate of caesareans are very high, and I don't want that at all.

WINDY: Is it your first child?

MEGHA: Yes, it is my first child. So that's something that I've been struggling with. There are two doctors: one doctor is only operating in a corporate hospital, and I looked at their rate card and it has all sorts of things that I don't want as an experience for my first birth; the other one has a small nursing home, but I'm not very sure if a hospital is the right place; so I have another option of a natural birthing centre. So there are three options.

WINDY: And are you familiar with the term 'stakeholder'?

MEGHA: Yeah.

WINDY: By stakeholder, apart from yourself, who else has a stake in this decision?

MEGHA: My husband.

WINDY: And what does he say?

MEGHA: That's probably the main issue, because he's fine for the natural birth, but the third option, which is a natural birthing centre, it's situated in Cochin, in Kerala, which is out of the state.

WINDY: And that's far away?

MEGHA: And that's far away, and his work will not permit him to probably take that many days, because he'll have to be there.

WINDY: So, in other words, if you go for that option, he won't be with you.

MEGHA: He will, but it'll be much more difficult. So, I am very pro that, and he is very iffy about that choice because of his work schedule.

WINDY: So, if he was supportive of you and if he said, 'Darling, anything you want and I can do it,' what would you do?

MEGHA: I'd just go to Cochin.

WINDY: So, you don't have a problem making a decision.

MEGHA: I guess.

WINDY: What do you mean you guess? Your face lit up.

MEGHA: I'm struggling with what choice to make then.

WINDY: OK. What's the issue with him? I thought you were going to say he couldn't attend the birth, and you said no. So, what would the actual situation be with him, if you took that option?

MEGHA: So, the situation would be that he may not be able to come … and we wouldn't obviously know when.

WINDY: Just finish your sentence there.

MEGHA: Yeah. He'll not be able to come in, probably, in time for the birth. There's a good chance.

WINDY: So, he might miss the birth?

MEGHA: Yeah, he might miss the birth. If he doesn't miss the birth and if he chooses to come two weeks earlier, but there is a chance that he may not be able to be there for the post care as much.

WINDY: So, he might miss the birth and he might even also, in addition, miss the post-birth care.

MEGHA: Yeah.

WINDY: OK, fine. But, if he didn't and if he was with you before the birth and the post-birth care, there'd be no problem.

MEGHA: Yeah.

WINDY: So the question is what's your stance towards him missing the birth and the post-birth care?

MEGHA: So I started with I don't want him to miss either. Now I'm stuck between somewhere making the choice, maybe.

WINDY: And what's his view on the subject?

MEGHA: He's not made a decision, and I think I'm struggling with getting him to make a decision on what ... also, apart from the fact that I'm struggling if this is the right decision at all, if I do take it.

WINDY: OK, so he's struggling to make a decision?

MEGHA: Yeah.

WINDY: What's he doing now? What's he saying now?

MEGHA: He wouldn't probably want to do that.

WINDY: He probably wouldn't want to do what?

MEGHA: He wouldn't want to go to Cochin, is his stance.

WINDY: So, his preference would be what?

MEGHA: Would be somebody here, somebody in Bombay.

WINDY: And your preference would be?

MEGHA: Would be Cochin.

WINDY: So the question is whether you do what you want against him, and possibly against you because you would ideally like him to be there at the birth and the pre-birth, or you go along with him and go against yourself.

MEGHA: Yeah.

WINDY: OK. Now do you have an emotional problem about doing this at all?

MEGHA: So I think I'm somewhere stuck that should I even be demanding this or if I am right to be demanding that he should be present with me in Cochin.

WINDY: Do you mean by demanding by saying to him, 'Look, darling, this is really, really, really, really, really important to me'?

MEGHA: Yeah.

WINDY: You give him the five. Do you know what the five is?

[By the 'five', I mean five 'reallys' which indicates the highest level of importance.]

MEGHA: No, I haven't given him the five.

WINDY: Give him the five which means there ain't no six; this is top billing.

MEGHA: OK.

WINDY: How many have you given him?

MEGHA: I think not much.

WINDY: You haven't even given him the one?

MEGHA: I have given him the one, one-and-a-half.

WINDY: Oh, the 'really, rea...'?

[Indicating one-and-a-half.]

MEGHA: Yeah.

WINDY: So what would happen if you gave him the five?

MEGHA: I think I'll feel guilty that I'm probably forcing him.

WINDY: OK, we'll come back to you in a minute. What would happen with him if you gave him the five?

MEGHA: ... He may get it.

WINDY: Yeah?

MEGHA: Yeah.

WINDY: You mean he understands how important it is or he would implement your wishes?

MEGHA: Yeah, I think he would work towards it.

WINDY: OK. So the thing that's stopping you is guilt then?

MEGHA: In some way, yeah.

WINDY: OK. Well there's another thing that's stopping you I can hear as well, because, if you get what you want, I'm going to insist that the middle name is Windy. Do you realise that (said with humour)?

MEGHA: OK.

WINDY: That's a deal. Right, what are you guilty about?

MEGHA: Of demanding this from him.

WINDY: Well, let's be clear about what you mean by demanding. Are you saying that, 'You absolutely have to do this, and I'm going to be disturbed against you if you don't,' or are you being very, very clear about what's really, really, really important to you?

MEGHA: ... [Pause] I want to be really, really clear about it, but somewhere I think is it getting mixed up with me being irrational somewhere and asking for too much?

WINDY: When you say 'asking for too much', what do you mean?

MEGHA: ...

WINDY: Because this is your first child, I assume that the child is wanted, and I guess, if we took a straw poll we would probably find out that having a first child is probably one of the peak experiences of a woman's life. So, somehow, if you really stress how important this is that you're being demanding. Of course, you're not allowed to be demanding because you're an REBT therapist, and we don't do that, so you've got to be rational about it (said with humour). I see that the tears are coming into your eyes. What's going on for you right now?

[Up to now I have been tracking what Megha has been saying and trying to understand the context of her problem as well as the nature of the problem itself. At this point it is becoming clear that she has downplayed the level of importance of having a natural birth because she sees being clear with husband that it is really, really, really, really, really important to her to have a natural childbirth as demanded.]

MEGHA: … [Pause]

WINDY: What just struck a chord with you?

MEGHA: … [Pause] Maybe it's not. … I don't know.

WINDY: Maybe it's not?

MEGHA: Maybe it's not too demanding.

WINDY: Maybe it's not too demanding?

MEGHA: Yeah.

WINDY: Yeah, and maybe it's perfectly possible to have something which is really, really, really, really, really important to you that's not a demand. And that realisation makes you feel what?

MEGHA: … [Long pause] Acceptance maybe.

WINDY: Yeah? OK. Now can you offer that acceptance to yourself?

MEGHA: … [Pause]

WINDY: Can you really show yourself that, 'I, Megha, can have something very, very, very important to me, one of the most important things that's been in my life so far, and that's not being demanding, and, if I really convey that to my husband, he will go along with it, and I can solve my problem'? Can you give yourself permission to really have strong, strong wishes and to express them, and accept yourself for doing that?

MEGHA: … [Pause]

WINDY: Or is there something in the way of doing that?

MEGHA: … It's a little difficult.

WINDY: What's difficult about it? I understand it's difficult. What's difficult about it?

MEGHA: ... [Long pause] Can I have a tissue?

[Megha is emotional at this point.]

WINDY: No, that's a bottle of water. Yeah. There you go. You get a flannel. Is that OK or would you rather have a tissue? Yeah, she wants a tissue. You don't need a flannel. You see, even here you get what you want. You asked for a tissue – no, we don't give you a bottle of water, nor do we give you a flannel, we give you a tissue. Alright?

[Megha has requested a tissue. One of the people in the group offers her a bottle of water and another a flannel. I use this to lighten the mood a little.]

MEGHA: Yeah.

WINDY: So what I'm saying to you, Megha, is what you really, really, really, really want is really, really, really important to you, and you can ask for that, and that brings the tears for you, but it's hard for you to really kind of digest that and act on it.

MEGHA: Yeah.

WINDY: Is that right? What's stopping you from doing that? What's stopping you from making you numero uno?

MEGHA: ... [Long pause] I don't know, maybe I think it's unfair.

WINDY: Unfair on whom?

MEGHA: On him.

WINDY: Well let's suppose it's unfair on him. Why does your husband have to be spared unfairness with this highly important thing that means so much for you?

MEGHA: ... [Long pause]

[Megha is still emotionally digesting the point that she can put herself first when something is centrally important to her. Given this, I pull back from questioning her rigid attitude that her husband has to be spared unfairness.]

WINDY: Because this is about putting you number one.

MEGHA: ... [Pause]

WINDY: Are there times when you've put him number one and his preferences?

MEGHA: ... I would say so.

WINDY: Yeah? Are there times when he puts you number one and your preferences?

MEGHA: Yeah, I would say so.

WINDY: OK. So he does that, right, and you do that. It sounds like it's a balance.

MEGHA: Yeah.

WINDY: So what is it about this issue that seems to be a bit of a difficulty, since you do have a history of doing that in your marriage?

MEGHA: ... [Pause] Maybe asking it of him.

WINDY: OK, so let's suppose you ask, what would you say?

MEGHA: What would he say?

WINDY: No, what would you say?

MEGHA: What would I say?

WINDY: Yeah.

MEGHA: To him?

WINDY: Yeah.

MEGHA: ... [Pause] This is really important for me.

WINDY: Sorry?

MEGHA: This is really important for me.

WINDY: Oh, you're using the one.

MEGHA: ... I guess I always use the one.

WINDY: You do, yeah. Well why don't you try the five? No commitment, let's try it here, right? I'll be your husband. Has he got hair (said with humour)?

[Laughter]

MEGHA: Yeah.

WINDY: So, imagine I'm your husband. What does he do for a living?

MEGHA: He's a voiceover artist.

WINDY: He's a voiceover artist. So, I've come back home from a heavy voiceover artist day, and I'm now ready to listen to my wife. And I want you to experiment using the five.

MEGHA: So ...

WINDY: Speak to me directly as if I were your husband.

MEGHA: OK ... [Pause] So we were going over the hospital thing, and I ... would like to make a decision on it, and I want to tell you that going to Cochin is really, really, really, really, really important for me, and I'd like ... you to ... say yes to that.

WINDY: OK. So how does that feel doing that?

MEGHA: ... I don't know. Unreal. I don't know.

WINDY: Unreal?

MEGHA: Yeah, I'm not convinced, I guess.

WINDY: You're not convinced by it?

MEGHA: Yeah.

WINDY: Really? OK, so what's not convincing by it?

MEGHA: I don't know.

WINDY: You missed out a 'really' or what?

MEGHA: No.

WINDY: What's not convincing for you?

MEGHA: ...

WINDY: By not convincing, you mean that that's not an accurate statement about what you want or that it is but you can't really accept it or you have some doubts and reservations about it? What do you mean by that?

MEGHA: I don't know if I'm able to fully express it.

WINDY: You mean because of the situation that we're in here or with your husband?

MEGHA: Maybe because of the situation here.

[Megha indicates that she is struggling with being assertive in this exercise because of the context of our conversation.]

WINDY: OK, but, if you really expressed it with your husband using the 'five reallys' approach, I might suggest that you say something like, 'Would you work with me on this?' or make it more of a joint decision, like it's a 'we' thing, rather than, 'This is what I want to do, will you agree?' If you did that, what do you think would happen?

[Despite her difficulty with being assertive in the exercise, I encourage Megha to do so in real life with her husband as she says that there is a good chance that he will agree once he understands how important having a natural birth is to her.]

MEGHA: ... I think there's a good chance he'll agree.

WINDY: OK, and how would you feel if he agreed?

MEGHA: … I'd be thrilled.

WINDY: OK, so are you willing to put this into practice tonight?

MEGHA: OK.

WINDY: Yeah?

MEGHA: Yeah.

WINDY: OK. And so you'll let us know what happens tomorrow?

MEGHA: I will.

WINDY: OK. So why don't you summarise what we've done, from your perspective?

MEGHA: … From my perspective, I think, for me, it was important to acknowledge that it's important for me.

WINDY: And at the level of importance that it truly is. … And what role did I play in that, do you think?

MEGHA: … To say it's OK that it's important to me.

[Mehga sees my main contribution was to suggest that it is OK to have a very important preference.]

WINDY: It's OK to have things that are really important to you and, if you really expressed it at that level, then it's something that your husband will probably agree with. Let's see.

MEGHA: Yeah.

WINDY: So … it's something about you starting to allow yourself to have things that are really important to you that you don't have to dilute your desires. Now, just on that point, whatever happens you're going to have this baby, and what would you want to teach the baby about the importance of their desires?

MEGHA: … That they can have … and he or she can have any desire, and they can express it, and it's important that they do.

WINDY: Yeah, you want to teach them that.

MEGHA: Yeah.

WINDY: OK. And so, I think a step towards that is to implement that in your own life, here and elsewhere, OK? It'll be interesting to see what he says.

MEGHA: Yeah.

[Later that month, I received the following email from Megha, "Just to update you, regarding the problem I had talked to you in our session, my husband and I have chosen Cochin, at last.). So, thank you for

curing me). I couldn't have asked for a better therapist at just the right and very important time in my life".]

Follow-up: seven months later[1]

The privilege of having a brief therapy session with Prof. Dryden came at a very opportune time for me as I was going through a dilemma which was to have a huge impact in my life – to have or not to have the birthing experience of my choice. When I look back, the therapy session was in itself short, simple and succinct. The deep respect and acceptance I felt of me, and my problem was itself very healing. I also realised with it, how I had not let myself accept how important the issue was for me. I marvel at the fact that in just those 15–20 minutes, my situation was understood deeply and accurately. Windy asked me important and pertinent questions to understand who or what was standing in my way to solve that problem. My inner guilt and resistance to accepting the extent to which that wish was important, was revealed in the conversation. When he pointed out the fact that this was my first pregnancy and becoming a parent is a momentous point in one's life, and thus I, of course, have the right to wish for the kind of birthing I wanted.

The other question which brought it home for me was about what would I tell my child about wishing for something and communicating that wish to a dear one. It was finally about communicating how important that wish was for me to my partner, which I did. I got the birth I wanted, an unmedicated, natural birthing experience and it was life-changing. But what was more life-changing were those 15 minutes, because they made me examine the many very very very very very important wishes I have had, that I have put away. So now, when I have a wish, I check it on the scale of one to five 'very's', which puts a lot of things in perspective for me. It has helped me in communicating my wishes so much easier because I now have clarity on how important that particular wish is to me. The feeling that I am asking for too much still persists even now, but now I know how to help myself with it.

Thank you, Windy, for your help. You played a huge and important role in supporting me in having the birth experience of my choice. My baby got the best and healthiest kind of beginning to his life because you helped me believe that it was ok that it was very very very very very important to me and that I could communicate it in that manner. I'll always be deeply grateful to you for that.

Note

1   See Appendix 2 for the email I sent to volunteers requesting a follow-up.

Chapter 8

Inappropriate behaviour

Overview

In this VBTC, which lasts for 17 minutes 18 seconds, Poorva raises an issue about a past incident where a male friend touched her inappropriately. She says that she has largely dealt with this issue and would lay down very firm boundaries if he tried to touch her inappropriately again. She also claims to have let go of her unhealthy anger towards the man. However, she questions whether she should or should not let go of this angry emotion and this is the focus of the conversation that follows. Poorva thinks that in letting this emotion go she is giving in or in some way communicating to the man that he can do what he wants to do, and that her anger would, in some way, prevent him from having such thoughts. In the interview, I help her to see that she can have a very strong preference about this man (and men in general) not thinking that it is OK to behave inappropriately to women, but very regretfully she does not have to have this preference met. She comes to see, at the end, that holding this flexible attitude and giving up her unhealthy anger does not mean that she is giving in or condoning such inappropriate male behaviour.

The VBTC

WINDY: OK, Poorva, what problem can I help you with today?

POORVA: So I will just give you a very brief background of what the problem is. About a year ago or so a certain friend, not a very close friend but a good friend, crossed his boundaries with me and touched me inappropriately. That is something I dealt with in a pretty short period of time, and I am OK.

WINDY: How did you deal with it?

POORVA: So, since I had learned REBT from Ma'am, and I was seeing Ma'am for therapy at that time, so I could understand that this is nothing to do with me, it is not my fault, I don't have to feel disgusted with my body. So, I dealt with it. Now the problem, as of today, with respect to this, is that I have actually come to a point of … at that point it was almost like, 'I hate this person, I would want that person dead,' etc., I have genuinely come to this thing of being OK with being in a social gathering, let's say at a wedding or something, around that person, and, even if he smiles at me or something, I can decently smile back and not feel a thing about it.

WINDY: Are you sure about that?

POORVA: Very sure about that. So, the issue is, it's a little weird, but it's almost like how can I let go of that anger?

WINDY: You still feel angry towards him?

POORVA: So I used to, which I don't now, because I feel like, OK, it can happen, I don't have to think of him as a terrible person or anything, what he did was very, very bad and that I would never let it happen again to me, and I can have all my boundaries with him – I can choose to not talk, I can choose to not communicate, I can choose to not be friends, but I don't have to think of him as a bad person.

WINDY: Right.

POORVA: So I've come to that now and I'm pretty comfortable with that. But, when I shared this with close friends, it's almost like, 'How can you do that? How can you let go of the anger?'

WINDY: So you've let go of the anger.

POORVA: Yeah.

WINDY: But your friends ask?

POORVA: So it's like a problem about the problem; how can I let go of the anger because it will probably mean that I'm giving in.

WINDY: You have let go of the anger or you haven't?

POORVA: I have.

WINDY: So you've solved your problem.

POORVA: Yes, that problem is solved.

WINDY: So what's your problem?

POORVA: Now the problem is that how can I let go of the anger, because I feel like somewhere it would mean that I'm letting that person know or feel that you can do what you want to.

WINDY: I can understand that, but you said you have already let go of your anger.

POORVA: Yes, I have.

WINDY: You've succeeded in doing it.

POORVA: Yes.

WINDY: And so when you say, 'How can I let go of it?'

POORVA: Yeah, in the sense I should not let go of it.

WINDY: Right, OK.

POORVA: I should not let go of it.

WINDY: Because letting go of it means that what?

POORVA: That I'm probably letting him know that he can do whatever he wants and I'll find a way to be OK with it. It's almost like giving in.

WINDY: OK. How does letting go of the anger mean that you are communicating to him that he can do whatever he wants and that he'll get away with it? Just help me to understand how that means?

POORVA: So, somehow, my actions around him. I'm very comfortable, even if he's there. Earlier, my expressions were the fact that I would not make any eye contact or, even if he would come, I'd probably go away. I don't know. I felt like that would, in a very indirect way, in a very passive-aggressive way let him know that, 'I hate what you did and I probably hate you also.' But now all those actions have changed. So, I am comfortable, I will be around, I don't have an issue, I'll even smile back if required.

WINDY: But you somehow think that, in doing that, he's more likely to?

POORVA: To believe that it's OK to do what he did.

WINDY: And so what is your concern? That he has that belief or that he might act on that belief?

POORVA: No, I don't think he'll act on that.

WINDY: So your concern is he's got that belief.

POORVA: Yeah.

WINDY: 'Well, she was OK with it, so I can do what I want. I'm not going to, but I could if I wanted to.' Is that what you're saying?

POORVA: … Yeah.

WINDY: You seem a bit hesitant there.

POORVA: Can you say it again for me?

WINDY: Well, if I can summarise, just so that I can make myself clear, that you have let go of your anger.

POORVA: Yes.

WINDY: But you think, in doing so, you've communicated something to this guy.

POORVA: Yes.

WINDY: What you've communicated to this guy is that he could cross the boundaries again, if he wanted to, and get away with it.

POORVA: Yeah.

WINDY: Now you don't think he will.

POORVA: No, no. I'm communicating to him that what he did back then was OK, because I'm OK with it.

WINDY: Yeah, because you haven't done what?

POORVA: ... OK, I'm confused.

WINDY: So how are you communicating that because you haven't said anything to him? It sounds like you haven't said to him, 'Listen, Fred, typical Indian name (said with humour) I don't hate you for what you did, but I want to make something very, very, very, very, very clear to you that what you did was completely out of order, and do not even think of doing it again because it isn't going to happen.'

POORVA: Yeah.

WINDY: You haven't had that conversation with him, have you?

POORVA: I have.

WINDY: You have?

POORVA: I have.

WINDY: So you've expressed clearly and directly.

POORVA: Very clear, yes.

WINDY: OK, so then you've done that, fine, and yet, in your mind there's a connection between holding your anger, and presumably we're talking about unhealthy anger where you hate him, because you can still be healthily angry – you can hate what he did but not him, but in your mind there's a connection between hating him, that kind of anger, and him somehow seeing that and seeing that you are not a person that he can approach. Even though you've told him that and he gets the message, somehow you connect your, if you like, healthy anger somehow gets through to him and he thinks, 'Oh, I can do it again. I'm not going to do it again, but I could do it again.'

POORVA: Yes.

WINDY: OK. Well, let's suppose that. Let's suppose the worst and, somehow, I don't know how it's going to happen, magically or whatever it is, but let's suppose that he's got a thought, 'Well, I could touch Poorva inappropriately, and I'm pretty sure that I could get away with it, I'm not going to but I could do that, even though she's told me, in no uncertain terms, that not to do it, I could do that.' Let's suppose that's what he thinks. How do you feel about him thinking that way?

POORVA: Disgusting. I feel disgusted by that. I can't let him think that, is what I think.

[Having given Poorva an opportunity to express herself and having clarified what she is saying, I think I am nearing the issue which is how Poorva handles the possibility of this man thinking that he could behave inappropriately with her again. Up to now she has thought that feeling anger prevents him from thinking that and adopting an acceptant stance would allow him to have these thoughts.]

WINDY: Because, if he thinks that, what?

POORVA: It would mean that I'm giving in. I don't have enough maybe self-respect or something of the sort.

WINDY: So, in some ways, you're giving in.

POORVA: Yeah.

WINDY: OK. You're giving into what?

POORVA: Giving into the belief that somebody can do that to someone else and they will be OK with it, or forget 'they', me, I will be OK with it.

WINDY: Yeah, so is he right or is he wrong?

POORVA: He's definitely wrong.

WINDY: He's wrong?

POORVA: Yeah.

WINDY: OK, now is he allowed to be wrong?

POORVA: Sure.

WINDY: In this case?

POORVA: Well, my heart says no but my head says yes.

[Poorva intellectually accepts that the man is allowed to be wrong, but emotionally she doesn't. This is common in REBT and I refer the reader to an early paper by Ellis (1963) on the subject. I choose to deal with this by having a conversation with her 'heart', the part of her that is having difficulty digesting what her head can digest.]

WINDY: OK, so let's have a word with your heart. So, heart, tell me why this guy is not allowed (said with humour)?

POORVA: Actually, no guy is allowed.

WINDY: No guy is allowed?

POORVA: Yeah.

WINDY: OK, so we're going to have to have a radical reboot of the whole of the human race, the male part of the human race (said with humour).

[Here, I use a vivid image of what Poorva's heart is calling for. My job is to help her to see that this is a legitimate preference and that she could either keep this flexible or make it rigid which I do a little later.]

POORVA: Yes.

WINDY: So a radical reboot, and, in this radical reboot, what would happen?

POORVA: That they would come to understand that you cannot cross boundaries with anybody, when and how you feel like it, and, if you do that, you ... you're just not good enough to be around.

WINDY: So how did you feel just then?

POORVA: When I said this?

WINDY: Yeah.

POORVA: Well, I believe what I said.

WINDY: How did you feel?

POORVA: In saying this?

WINDY: Yeah.

POORVA: Frankly speaking, right now nothing.

[I thought I detected a change in affect in Poorva which I enquired about, but did not pursue when she responded in the negative. In general, changes in affect are important to explore as they may indicate the presence of important issues or moments of change.]

WINDY: OK. So, if you stand back and look at what you want, which is a radical reboot of the male species, which is great, I'm not against that, but does it have to happen or doesn't it have to happen?

POORVA: Just because it's what I want, it's not going to happen.

WINDY: Does your heart believe that?

POORVA: It definitely believes that.

WINDY: It doesn't have to happen.

POORVA: Because that is not how most men function.

WINDY: It doesn't have to happen.

POORVA: Yeah. I would love for it to happen.

WINDY: So he's allowed to think what he wants.

POORVA: Eventually, yes.

[Poorva's statement here is interesting. The man in question is allowed to think what he wants, but only 'eventually'. I pick up on this.]

WINDY: No, now. Why, right now, isn't he allowed the wrong belief about you as a woman and this representation of why aren't men allowed to have this belief? I'm not saying it's right or wrong, it's definitely wrong. Why aren't they allowed to think wrong thoughts and hold wrong attitudes about you in this case and, generally, women?

POORVA: When you put it that way, I do understand because they are people and they are going to have …

WINDY: I'm sorry, what did you say?

POORVA: Because they are people.

WINDY: What was that? What was that word?

[I again use my 'hard of hearing' technique to draw her attention to an important point.]

POORVA: Because they're human beings.

WINDY: They're human beings.

POORVA: Yes.

WINDY: Men are human beings.

POORVA: They're allowed to think.

WINDY: OK, so men are human beings, and this man is a human being. What follows from that?

POORVA: Can I say that they're not allowed but they still might, and that's OK because they're human beings?

WINDY: You can say what you like.

POORVA: Yeah, so that makes me feel better.

WINDY: OK, you're still saying, 'They're not allowed, but they might.'

POORVA: But they still might, yeah.

WINDY: Yeah, OK.

POORVA: And that's OK.

WINDY: OK. So what would stop you from going the whole hog and saying they're allowed? Somehow what does that mean?

POORVA: It feels like, if I say that they're allowed, it's almost like saying, 'OK, do whatever you like. You can just touch anyone, do whatever you like,' and it wouldn't mean anything.

*[Poorva is still resisting the idea that men are allowed to **think** wrongly about touching women inappropriately because she sees that in doing so she is giving them license to **behave** inappropriately towards women.]*

WINDY: How does it follow that, because in your mind you're saying, 'This is very, very wrong, but, unfortunately, men, and this man doesn't have to do what I want which means that it is impossible for them to think about this.' That's what it means, the idea that, once you allow them, you're really saying, 'Sadly, regretfully, times five, while I want men not to be able to think about that, but that doesn't mean that they must not. They might, and, therefore, I can't stop them from thinking what they want. I'd like to.' I'd like to have a little clicker that would say, 'Oh man, gone,' but, unfortunately, they may have a little clicker saying, 'Woman, can.' So, if you go the whole hog and say, 'Yeah, it is very, very unfortunate … I may want them not to be able to, but, by allowing them, I'm not giving in, I'm just saying, unfortunately, my wishes don't have to be,' because I would like a world where it's impossible for men to think this way, and maybe, on the planet Poorva, we can redesign such men.

POORVA: Sure.

WINDY: Yeah?

POORVA: Yeah, that appeals to me.

WINDY: That appeals to you?

POORVA: Yes.

WINDY: But, on planet Earth, what happens?

POORVA: What you said that, unfortunately, regretfully, etc., I may not want it, but, yes, they are still allowed.

WINDY: Yeah.

POORVA: And it wouldn't mean anything. The meanings I'm attaching – that it would then mean that I'm letting go and giving in – it wouldn't mean that.

[Once Poorva allows herself to have very strong preferences and to keep these flexible, she sees that the meanings she had been giving to allowing men to think inappropriately are no longer true.]

WINDY: That's right, yeah, because you're really saying, 'I have to get the kind of world that I want, which is a world where men find it impossible to think these things about women, and, because

I can't get that way, somehow I'm contributing to this world by giving in,' etc.

POORVA: Yes, that's exactly what it always is.

WINDY: Yeah, but if you really show yourself that, really, 'No,' you could really have, again, a very, very, very strong preference, but do we have any cod liver oil, because this is a cod liver oil moment, isn't it?

POORVA: Yeah, it is.

WINDY: And it is really saying, 'I really want a world where men, this man in particular, can't even think that they could abuse somebody and get away with it, but, sadly, regretfully, it doesn't have to be that way. But, if I was in charge of the universe, it would be this way.'

POORVA: Yes.

WINDY: So I guess you should have a word with the people who are responsible for the design of mankind, and I'm using the word 'mankind' advisedly, 'MANkind'. So that's your homework assignment, to have a word with the deity or whoever it is, and make an application for that kind of design modification (said with humour). So why don't you summarise what we've done today?

POORVA: ... I guess when the regretfully and unfortunately were added to the statement.

WINDY: Times five.

POORVA: Times five yes, I can say that they're allowed. Earlier, to even say it, just to utter the words that they're allowed was not OK, but I guess, if I do what you said and practise it a little, it could become easier.

WINDY: Yeah, and also, I don't know if it helps, but, in reality, they, again regretfully and unfortunately, allow themselves, right?

POORVA: Right.

WINDY: And it would be great if they didn't, and maybe we should have all kinds of educational programmes, etc., but the thing is that you're quite clear that, if he starts acting on this, you cut it off.

[On reading the transcript, I think I could have stressed more the importance of having educational programmes designed to address the male thinking to which Poorva rightly objects, but the main thrust of my intervention would have been the same: to help Poorva see that she could

have a very strong preference that men would not have such thoughts, but sadly and regretfully it does not follow that they must not do so.]

POORVA: Yeah, absolutely.

WINDY: Right. So, if you allow him, in your mind, to have these very negative thoughts, and you're clear that you don't … add all the unfortunately's and regretfully's that you can … then, as I say, go and have a word with the designer of mankind, because, unfortunately, your silent wishes aren't doing it. Maybe you're not concentrating hard enough. Let's try an experiment: 'I really … is he still thinking? No, I'm not it hard enough' (said with humour).

POORVA: I'm not going to do that.

WINDY: No? Why aren't you going to do that?

POORVA: Because that's silly.

WINDY: Because, it's silly. Ok, let's stop and get their views.

Follow-up: Seven Months Later[1]

What I liked / did not like about the experience?

The session with Dr Dryden was extremely enriching. Honestly, I liked every bit of the experience. There is nothing unlikeable that I can think of.

What did you learn from the session?

In the problem discussed, I was feeling guilty about having let go of the felt anger towards someone who had behaved unfairly according to me. It felt like I must hold on to this anger because it gave a false sense of control and letting it go somehow got equated with 'losing' an imaginary battle. While knowing how irrational this kind of magical thinking is, it was still hard to be rational about it because it served some odd protective purpose. I replayed my session with Dr Dryden in my head later on, and the following were my learnings –

1. *Demands of fairness need to be worked on because however 'unfair' people may seem, there are no such standards to gauge either.*
2. *I need to work on other acceptance. In the context of my problem, my mind equated accepting the other with 'being ok with unacceptable behaviour from the other'. The distinction between these two concepts got clarified during the session.*

3. I learnt that however valid a feeling or a thought might seem, how-
    ever valid it may seem to expect fairness, however valid it may
    seem to want people to not behave in certain ways, it doesn't have
    to be so. The seeming validity of the demand is not directly propor-
    tional to its chances of working out the way one wants. Thus, an
    expectation is a much functional alternative!
4. My BIGGEST take away was – 'I'd prefer for people to respect
    other's boundaries, but sadly and unfortunately they don't have to'.
    Sadly and unfortunately, they don't have to.

Did you solve your problem after the session? To what extent do you still have the problem?

My problem got solved very much during the session. I don't see myself
having the problem anymore. I tried to think if I sometimes struggle
again with the same feelings in my present life, but I cannot recall such
occasions. It is pretty great because I think I've found an almost per-
manent solution to a problem I long struggled with.

What use, if any, did you make of what you learned in your life subsequent to the session?

I had learnt about unconditional other acceptance only in theory so far.
This session was the first time that I experienced unconditional other
acceptance in 'emotion', reaching far beyond theory. This is one of the
qualities I am genuinely trying to inculcate, as I feel it could make me
a better therapist.

Did you apply what you learned to other areas of your life? If so, please explain.

I am actively trying to work on my demands of fairness from people in
general.

Please describe Professor Dryden's role in the session. What was helpful and not helpful about his contribution to the session?

I prefer not to get carried away by concepts such as luck / destiny and
the like as they make way for passivity in my case, and I make sure not

to be carried away. However, to be able to have a session (even if brief) with Dr Dryden seemed to be like a huge stroke of positive luck. Dr Dryden's choice of words during the session and his accurate analysis of the problem (which I thought I was aware of until he guided me to it) was his most helpful contribution to the session. I had attempted to work through the discussed problem in various ways earlier. But his words, which validated my feelings alongside showing me that although valid, it is still unhealthy to think that way is what has stayed with me even months after the session. His validation of feelings using the words 'sadly and unfortunately it doesn't have to be so', will almost always stay with me.

If you requested the recording and transcript of the session, what use did you make of them?

I, unfortunately, have not requested for the transcript yet.

Note

1   See Appendix 2 for the email I sent to volunteers requesting a follow-up.

Chapter 9

Lack of support

Overview

In this VBTC which lasts for 25 minutes 32 seconds, M wants help for her feelings of hurt about a friend not supporting her and showing that he cared enough for her when others attacked her integrity. I help her to develop and hold a flexible attitude towards this which would encourage her to try to pin the friend down so that he would account for his lack of support. I also help her to see that while it is important for her to get this statement from him, he does not have to give it. In which case, her flexible attitude towards the resultant lack of (interpersonal) resolution would serve as her (intrapersonal) resolution.

The VBTC

WINDY: OK, M, how can I help you today?

M: So, I'm going to have to go back to one-and-a-half years back.

WINDY: OK, let's do that.

M: The thing was … there were a few people who I knew, and you can say there was both a professional relationship and there was a personal relationship, which developed slowly and gradually. I guess none of us expected it to develop like that. It was going smoothly and all of those things, but then there were certain things that came up, and I honestly don't know what exactly happened, but there was a lot of politics coming in, and all the back-biting started. That person was actually an authority figure.

WINDY: The person that you became friends with, you mean?

M: Yeah, it went onto a level where he started seeing me as his child.

WINDY: Child?

M: Yeah.

WINDY: How old is he?

M: He is around 52. So, we developed that relationship.

WINDY: So, it turned into like a father ...

M: Father and daughter.

WINDY: From his perspective?

M: From my perspective too.

WINDY: As well?

M: Yeah.

WINDY: OK.

M: But, I don't know, there were some restrictions from his side. I don't know what it was, but there was a time when he actually would have had to stand up, but he didn't stand up for me.

WINDY: Stand up for you for what?

M: I would say in defence.

WINDY: Of what?

M: There were certain workplace things that were going on.

WINDY: And you were looking to him for?

M: I thought he would because I honestly didn't know from where the problem started coming out. It was like I experienced that whole phase of being targeted over there. I experienced it.

WINDY: Targeted over?

M: In that workplace.

WINDY: Not about your relationship with this guy, about something else.

M: Yeah.

WINDY: OK.

M: But it just happens that he's the figure; he's the authority in that workplace.

WINDY: And so, he could've intervened and supported you.

M: Yeah, he could have.

WINDY: But he didn't.

M: Yeah. And things took a bad turn, and I, at that time, was emotionally drained because you can say my integrity was targeted.

WINDY: By?

M: I wouldn't be comfortable in saying.

WINDY: No, by a person.

M: Yeah.

WINDY: OK. So, a person or several people?

M: There were three or four people involved.

WINDY: OK, so three or four people were targeting you and questioning your integrity.

M: Yeah.

WINDY: OK. And this guy could've intervened and stood up for you, but he didn't.

M: Yeah.

WINDY: OK. Listen, I don't want you to name names at all, but I just want to get a sense of what we're talking about here.

M: So ... after certain months, I took a stand and I started maintaining my distance and I got out of the whole thing.

WINDY: That was your stand to maintain a distance?

M: No, I mean I was like, 'I need to get out of it, let me just get out of it.'

WINDY: You mean leave?

M: Leave everything.

WINDY: Leave the job.

M: Yeah.

WINDY: OK.

M: So I did that, and I left with a lot of hurt in me that things happened that way. I didn't expect it to happen that way. After that, I never got in touch. Nothing happened. I was completely cut off from those people, even from that person.

WINDY: When you say 'cut off', you mean you cut yourself off or you were cut off by them?

M: It was kind of I cut myself off from them. I chose not to be in that circuit.

WINDY: Right, because of hurt?

M: Because of hurt.

WINDY: OK.

M: And it just so happens that, after a couple of months, I was indirectly pushed back in that same circle.

WINDY: Indirectly pushed back? I'm dying to ask why or how.

M: I will tell you that it's another personal thing.

[It is clear that M does not want to be specific and I wish to respect this, so the conversation will be more general than I would have liked.]

WINDY: Fine, OK.

M: So the issue is I have to face that person.

WINDY: This is the guy.

M: That same figure, but I can't get myself to be normal. Whenever I see that person, I feel the anger and the hurt that I had experienced a long way back.

WINDY: So, the anger and the hurt, mainly the hurt but also the anger is actually preventing you from doing this? Is that what you're saying?

M: ... Yeah, kind of.

WINDY: You seem doubtful about that.

M: It's like there's a lot of ... It's like I have to do certain things, but the anger, the sadness doesn't let me do it the way I would normally do it.

WINDY: OK, so, again, the anger and the hurt and sadness are preventing you from doing what you want to do, which is what? What do you want to do?

M: So it's like I have to fulfil some responsibilities in regards to what I'm currently doing, but ... it prevents me to do it as comfortably as I would want to do it, because I'm dealing with the same person.

WINDY: OK. So are you doing it, but uncomfortably?

M: Yes.

WINDY: But you are doing it?

M: Yeah.

WINDY: So it's not stopping you from doing it.

M: Yeah, I feel that I hold myself back at certain times, but I can't, after a point; I still have to get my way out and do those certain things.

WINDY: Which you do eventually or you don't?

M: Yeah, and I also try to find other people to get it done.

WINDY: Right, OK, so rather than ...

M: I, myself.

WINDY: And what you want to do is to what?

M: I want to comfortably be able to do all of those things.

WINDY: And what conditions would have to exist for you to do that?

M: ... I guess I want some resolution coming from that side also that looks to see what happened. I just want my answers to come out from there, why it happened.

WINDY: So you're waiting for him to make the first move.

M: I have asked that person that but I still don't have my answers.

WINDY: What have you said?

M: I have asked him that, 'I don't know what your side of the situation was, but, if you tell me what your situation was, maybe it gets easier for me to deal with all of it, because I honestly have gone through a lot with that thing.'

WINDY: So does he know that you felt very hurt?

M: And probably he gives me a thing that, 'I will not tell you anything because you're going to be hurt. Why do you want to go back in the past?' And my thing is I'm still there with it.

WINDY: OK, so you're stuck in the past.

M: Yeah.

WINDY: And you're looking towards him for some statement so you can get some resolution, but he won't do that because he predicts that you'll feel hurt. And what do you say to that when he says that?

M: So I am, anyway, still holding onto it; I'm still not out of it.

WINDY: Yeah, so he's right; you would be hurt. Is that right?

M: I don't know what story he'll give me, so I just want to know the fact ...

WINDY: Well, he predicts that the story isn't going to be a good one because it's going to be hurtful to you. So what would you like from me?

[Up to now, I have let M tell me the problem from her perspective. I now ask for her goal.]

M: I, basically, want to deal with that feeling of being sad and angry, because I really want a lot against him, and I give it back also, but it still doesn't come out.

WINDY: OK. So let me be clear, because sometimes hurt comes into the picture, sometimes it comes out, sometimes anger comes in. So you've got three feelings: anger, sadness and hurt. Which do you think is the biggest block for you to at least get some resolution that you're looking for?

[I was expecting M to target hurt for change, but she omitted it altogether. So I listed the three emotions that she had mentioned and asked her which was the biggest block.]

M: I think the hurt.

WINDY: OK, hurt. OK, so what are you most hurt about?

M: About being the support that he could've been and not being it.

WINDY: So you're most hurt about the fact that he didn't give you support that you, what?

M: That I expected.

WINDY: Why did you expect that?

M: Because I told you we had that relationship; I actually saw him over there.

WINDY: So, given the relationship that you had, you expected him to do that, and the fact that he didn't do that, it's hurtful to you because it meant what?

M: ... It meant it was important to me.

WINDY: Right, it was important to you and he didn't recognise that it was that important to you. So, you see, one of the dynamics of hurt, what people are hurt about, is that people recognise that the other person may not be as invested in the relationship as you are, and it sounds like you were invested in a father and daughter relationship, and you expected your father figure to be supportive, to stand up for you, to protect you, and his failure to do that meant maybe the relationship wasn't as important to him as it was to you.

[I decide at this point to offer M my understanding of the hurt-related adversity because I am aware that time is at a premium.]

M: But I'll question him that also. He still claims it was very important, and that's what I don't understand.

WINDY: OK, so let me ask you a question. I'll put this in a different context. Do you think it's best to judge a man by what he says or for what he does?

M: I guess does.

WINDY: Right, and you know that, and so you're not buying what he says, because you know you've judged the man by his actions, and that's what the hurtful thing is; that he has shown you that he didn't care enough about you or he was a negligent father, and you really wanted him to be a caring father. OK, so what's your goal in talking this to me? How would you like to deal with that adversity, because it is an adversity? There's nothing I can change to make that pain free. The fact that he wasn't as invested in the relationship as you were, and as you hoped him to be, and he also might tell you various things that might reinforce that, because that's what he's saying to you. He says, 'If I tell you the real reason, you're going to feel hurt.' He's actually showing that he's protecting you, in a way, but you're more invested in actually finding out, aren't you? So what's your goal? How would you like to handle that emotionally, given the fact that it is an adversity for you?

M: ... I think I'm just a little too much affected. Now that I know it doesn't matter, it shouldn't be mattering to me, I've grown, I've got out of it, but ...

[Part of M's difficulty is that she is not clear about her goal and believes that it shouldn't matter to her when it clearly does.]

WINDY: But everything that you've said to me today indicates that it still matters to you. And have you found it effective to try to convince yourself that it shouldn't matter to you?

M: ...

WINDY: Is that good? Have you found that a useful strategy?

M: ... I don't see it working.

WINDY: No, and do you know why? Because it's a lie. It really does matter to you, and, in a way, it should matter to you because it does matter to you. So let's go back to my question. OK, let me put a suggestion: what if I could help you to get an emotion that was ... reflective of the fact that this is an important thing, reflective of the adversity that you faced, and was still painful because the event was painful, but would enable you to have a different type of discussion with him and maybe allow you to hear what he has to say, and to tell him that, 'OK, tell me. I may find it painful, but tell me'? How about if I helped you to get such an emotion?

[I realise that I need to take more of a lead to help M set a goal, so I use REBT's concept of a healthy negative emotion to spell out what this would involve for M.]

M: I would love it.

WINDY: Yeah? What would you call that emotion? I mean I've got a name for it, but what would you call it?

M: I would call it my satisfaction because I got my answer from it.

WINDY: Yeah, but I'm talking about what would you call the emotion about the adversity, about the fact, let's assume, that this guy didn't care enough about you to support you? What would that emotion be that wasn't hurt; that was still negative, but would allow you to go forward rather than hold yourself back and be quite honest with him and invite him to talk to you, knowing that you could take whatever he said, but still not like it of course? What would you call that emotion?

M: ... I'm just blank. Honestly, I'm blank.

WINDY: OK, so do you want to hear my version of it? To feel sad and sorrowful but not hurt. How would you feel about if I could help you to feel sad and sorrowful but not hurt? But you'd still feel sad and sorrowful. I can't help you to do that, nor am I going to try to. Do you know why?

M: Because it needs to just come out?

WINDY: Because this is something which is important to you and was an adversity, right? So are you ready? Are you sure? OK, so let's review what we know and what we don't know. We know that you feel hurt, we know that you see that this guy didn't support you in the way that you expected him to support you, which indicates that maybe he didn't see the relationship as important to him as you did, and that your preference would've been for him to support you. We know that. Is that right? Is that correct? OK. And we know that you were hurt. What we don't know is whether your hurt was based on Attitude 1 or Attitude 2. So listen very carefully as I go over Attitude 1. These are attitudes that not necessarily would be going on in your mind, but attitudes that really explain your hurt and perhaps explain the fact that I could help you to feel sorrowful but not hurt, OK?

So, 'I really wanted him to support me and to show that he cared, but, sadly and regretfully, he didn't have to do that,' or, 'I really wanted him to support me and show that he cared and, therefore, he absolutely should've done that.' Which was your hurt based on?

[Having helped M to set feeling sad and sorrowful rather than hurt as an emotional goal, I use my WRAP method (see Chapter 2) to help her to identify the attitude that underpinned her feelings of hurt and the attitude that would underpin her goal-related feeling of what I call hurt-free sorrow – see the following.]

M: The second one.

WINDY: That's right. What would you feel if you really believed the first one?

M: The first one?

WINDY: Yeah.

M: At least the intensity of what I'm going through now, it wouldn't have been that bad.

WINDY: OK, and I think you'd feel what I call hurt-free sorrow.

M: Hurt-free sorrow, yeah.

WINDY: It's still going to be painful, but it's going to be sorrowful and you're going to feel sad. So, let's see how to get there. When you stand back and look at those two attitudes, where one is saying, 'I really wish that he had supported me and showed he cared, but, sadly and regretfully, he didn't have to,' and, 'I really wished he'd supported me and showed me he cared and, therefore, he absolutely should've done that,' as you stand back and look at it, which do you think is the healthiest one for you?

[Here I am using my choice-based method of dialectical examination of her rigid and flexible attitudes (see Chapter 2).]

M: … Maybe the first one.

WINDY: Which was what?

M: Which was that he could've, but, regretfully, he didn't.

WINDY: Yeah, and that he didn't have to.

M: He didn't have to.

WINDY: OK. That's right, because that would enable you to do what?

M: … He just read his role.

WINDY: No, now, what would that enable you to do?

M: …

WINDY: If you really believed that, 'I really wanted him to do this but he didn't have to do that, really,' because who knows why, and we may need to find out, would it enable you to go away from him or towards him and actually really pin him down, because it sounds like you really haven't pinned him down?

M: Yeah, I want to pin him down.

WINDY: But pin him down in a healthy way. We don't want any rugby tackles or wrestling; not that kind of 'pinned down' (said with humour). I'm talking about you telling him, 'Look, tell me, be honest, I'm not going to like it, sure, but I can take it.' Can you see that that attitude will help you to do that, because the attitude of, 'He absolutely should've done it,' is helping you to either be hurt or to almost attack him? Which do you think is true, by the way: that he absolutely should've done … what you wanted him to do and support you; or, sadly and regretfully, he didn't have to do it? Which do you think is consistent with the world as you now see it?

M: The second one: regretfully not.

WINDY: Yeah. And which is more sensible, do you think?

M: The second one.

WINDY: What would you be reluctant to give up about the first one? What would it mean to you to give up the idea that, 'I live in a world where my expectations about how this guy was going to support me didn't have to be granted, even though I really wanted it to be granted'? What would it mean to you to give that up, that it has to be this way, and to get the idea that it didn't have to be this way? Do you feel any resistance to giving up that idea?

[Here I am looking for any doubts, reservations and objections that M might have about giving up her rigid attitude about not getting support and caring from her friend.]

M: Slightly, but, now that I think about it, it's just better that I just do it.

WINDY: Yeah, that's right.

M: So, even though my resistance would've been what I felt, I would take the effort to get myself. I know I can push myself.

WINDY: So, if you prepare yourself for a discussion and really show yourself that, 'Yes, he did let me down, I did have expectations, he didn't meet that, but, sadly and regretfully, – cod liver oil – the world doesn't have to be as I want it to be. And then I'm going to go to him, from that mindset, and I'm going to say to him, "Look, I want to hear. Don't worry, I can take it. Tell me."' Then he'll either tell you or not. What do you predict that he might say? Any idea?

M: Whatever he's been doing until now by not telling me, and telling me that it's just stupid of me to think about the past, and that I'm just playing with my health by thinking of it.

WINDY: OK, and you could say, 'No, I'm not playing with the past, I'm dealing with the present, and the present is I want you to now, in the present, tell me why you didn't support me.' Now you can't make him say that. Let's suppose, even after you showing him all these things, he still decides not to do that. Now how are you going to feel?

M: I think I will feel that sense of frustration or something. I am making the effort and I am not getting to where I want to get.

WINDY: That's right, and you know why?

M: ... Because it's not that important?

WINDY: No, it is important to you. Do you know why?

M: ... Because, for him, it's not that important, I guess.

WINDY: No. We don't know. Because that's what happens on the planet Earth sometimes (said with humour). On the planet M, it will say, 'Bloody hell, I don't want to tell this woman, but a strange force is making me' (again said with humour). So, first of all, you need to be prepared to go into the situation by reminding yourself that, sadly and regretfully, he didn't have to show that this relationship was as important to him in the sense of him supporting you. So that will get you into the situation. You need to be direct and, if he says, 'It's in the past,' say that it's in the present, so you pin him down in that sense, but still allow for the fact that he might not tell you, and he doesn't have to. If he does tell you, then you could utilise that same philosophy, which is that you can deal with it in terms of what he does. But you do need to prepare yourself for the possibility that he may not tell you.
So do you want to summarise where we've got to?

M: ... That he should have, but, regretfully, he's not done it.

WINDY: Ideally he should have.

M: Ideally he should have and, regretfully, he didn't do it.

WINDY: And nor does he have to.

M: Nor does he have to.

WINDY: Don't forget that.

M: And I kind of have to ask him in a very different way the same thing and be prepared for still not getting the answer and still dealing with it, but he's not going to probably tell me about it.

WINDY: That's right, and the way to resolve that is to ask yourself would you like a resolution to this, do you need it? Or would you like it but you don't need it?

M: ... [Pause] I may not need it, but I'd like it.

WINDY: And that's your resolution. Strangely enough, you can come to a resolution by showing yourself that you don't need a resolution, because, if you believe yourself that you need a resolution, you're going to pick at it, pick, pick, pick. This is what you've been doing. Anything else you want to bring up about this or are we done?

M: I think I'm happy with what just happened.

WINDY: OK, then, thank you very much.

Follow-up: seven months later[1]

The interview aptly focused on my needs and helped me gain clarity towards the solutions I was seeking. As a student, I realised and observed how effortlessly Professor Dryden demonstrated the process. As an individual simply just dealing with an issue I felt very comfortable all through the session. The interview helped gain an insight into the blocks that I was experiencing in order to deal effectively with the issue.

After the interview, I definitely felt more confident to face the situation and was relaxed as I had felt he absolutely understood the turmoil I was experiencing and helped me look into the matter with different perspectives.

I did make use of the suggestions, after which the problem doesn't seem to trouble me to the extent it did earlier.

Note

1   See Appendix 2 for the email I sent to volunteers requesting a follow-up.

Chapter 10

Disrespect

Overview

In this VBTC lasting 19 minutes and 12 seconds, Mrinmaye Sen discusses what she introduces as her anger problem with being disrespected. The assessment and intervention sections of this conversation are fairly straightforward in that, using an example with her boss, I helped Mrinmaye Sen to identify and examine her rigid attitude towards being disrespected and to develop a flexible attitude as an alternative. What is more challenging for me is helping Mrinmaye Sen to see that her goals of being instantly unbothered about the adversity of disrespect are problematic and that it is healthy to struggle towards feeling annoyed or healthily angry about the adversity. The interview also brings out that a person can be inclined to cling to a rigid attitude because of its perceived usefulness. My approach to this in Mrinmaye Sen's case is to help her see that it is the preference component of the rigid attitude that is helpful and not the rigid component and that this preference component is also present in the flexible attitude. Thus, she can let go of her commitment to the rigid attitude without losing anything.

The VBTC

WINDY: OK, Mrinmaye Sen, what stress problem can I help you with this evening?

MRINMAYE SEN: So I'm doing reasonably well in my life, and I have learnt to inculcate a pleasant personality in myself.

WINDY: You'll have to teach me how you did that (said with humour).

MRINMAYE SEN: Sure. You have no idea how thrilled I'd be to get free extra time with you. So, largely, people like me and, largely, I make friends easily. Now my problem is, if somebody of power or somebody criticises my work, I will definitely, while I'm facing that person, not let that person know that it's disturbed me, but deep inside I'd be not feeling OK about it.

WINDY: Right, OK. What do you do for a living?

MRINMAYE SEN: I'm a psychologist.

WINDY: You're a psychologist, OK. And so, if your work is criticised, for example, you are privately disturbed about that. What emotion do you experience?

MRINMAYE SEN: … Anger. Some amount of anger.

WINDY: Towards whom?

MRINMAYE SEN: Towards the person.

WINDY: Towards the person, OK. So, you're angry towards them. And is this anger helpful or unhelpful, would you say?

MRINMAYE SEN: … No, it's definitely not helpful, because for the next couple of hours it'll be in my mind quite actively. Even the next day I might think about it for a couple of times.

WINDY: So, you ruminate for a while, but then, after a day, you let it go.

MRINMAYE SEN: Right.

WINDY: So, what's your goal in bringing this issue up with me? What would you like to take away with you?

MRINMAYE SEN: Right. My goal would be, right from the very beginning I'm able to let go of it; I'm able to talk myself out of the situation, but I want to do it quickly.

WINDY: How quickly?

MRINMAYE SEN: Maybe it might take me a day's time.

WINDY: And you'd like to be able to do it in how quick a time?

MRINMAYE SEN: Maybe instantly. Maybe not let it bother me in the first place.

WINDY: Well I can't help you to do that. Do you know why?

MRINMAYE SEN: No.

WINDY: Because it's important to you. It's important for you not to be criticised.

MRINMAYE SEN: Yes.

WINDY: So, you are going to be bothered about it. The question is how can I help you to feel healthily bothered about it. If you manage to do this instantly, you can teach me how to do it, because I haven't managed to do it yet (said with humour). I haven't quite got the instant thing. I can help you to do it reasonably quickly. I can certainly help you not to spend a day. Incidentally, after a day has passed and you've come out of this and you look back at it, what's your feeling about being criticised, when you have come out of this rumination? How do you then feel about it?

[In my view Mrinmaye Sen has an unrealistic goal: to be instantly not bothered about it. There are two problems about this: the instant aspect and the not bothered aspect, both of which I address. In addition, I am thinking at this point to what extent her anger towards the other is ego-defensive in nature meaning that she is angry to defend the attack on her self-esteem.]

MRINMAYE SEN: So, when I've sorted it out how do I feel afterwards?
WINDY: Yeah.
MRINMAYE SEN: How do I feel afterwards? Then I still have the negative feeling but it's reasonably less.
WINDY: What's the negative feeling?
MRINMAYE SEN: … I'm not able to find a name for the emotion, but it's a little bit of regret maybe or maybe I'm a little upset with that person but I'm willing to accept that person.
WINDY: OK, so it's still an anger, particularly the last bit. I'm not sure what you're regretful about, but we'll leave that alone for a minute. So, you're still a little upset with the person, but you've let it go. How did you manage to do that?
MRINMAYE SEN: I tell myself that it's alright, I can actually tolerate it. There are more other things that I need to focus myself on. This is not the only issue. There are too many other things that are waiting for my attention.
WINDY: So, you're able to put it into a wider framework. Is that right?
MRINMAYE SEN: Yeah.
WINDY: But do you think that you're really dealing with the anger issue? What would happen if I helped you to deal with the anger issue earlier? Would you like that?

[In a VBTC, it is important to see how a person has already tried to deal with the problem and build on that, if possible. In doing this I ask myself has the person dealt with their major adversity? In Mrinmaye Sen's case she has, in my view, helped herself, to some degree, by putting the event into a wider context, but she has not dealt with the main

adversity, which I have yet to discover. We then go on to deal with a specific example of the problem.]

MRINMAYE SEN: Yes.

WINDY: Let's see what you're angry about. So, when this person criticises you, who is it?

MRINMAYE SEN: It could be anybody. Let's say my boss.

WINDY: He or she?

MRINMAYE SEN: She.

WINDY: And she says what as an example of criticism?

MRINMAYE SEN: Like a recent episode happen, I asked for permission from her to do a workshop. I asked her, 'Can I do a workshop in our setting?' She said, 'No, don't do it this week, do it next week.' So, I said, 'I really need to do it this week. It's pretty important. I'll do another workshop next week, let me do it this week.' This was a message exchange we were having over WhatsApp. So, she said, 'Listen, if I've told you no, you should not be asking me this question again,' and that very instant I had this surge of negativity towards her.

WINDY: So, what about that were you most angry about?

MRINMAYE SEN: I felt that my request was too small. In any case, she need not be so curt.

WINDY: So, somehow, you took that as meaning that your request was unimportant?

MRINMAYE SEN: No, but I felt that she was probably looking down upon me. That was what I was taking it as. She was not giving me a significant amount of importance, because I made a small request, she is cutting it down.

WINDY: OK, and you also were kind of angry with her curtness.

MRINMAYE SEN: Yes.

WINDY: Which do you think is the real issue: the looking down on you or the curtness?

MRINMAYE SEN: ... I think it's looking down on me.

[There are two adversities in Mrinmaye Sen's account. I highlight these for her and ask what is the real issue which is 'her boss looking down on her'. This strengthens my view that Mrinmaye Sen is experiencing ego-defensive anger – see Appendix 1.]

WINDY: I think so too. So ... how do you feel about you when she looked down on you in that moment? Let's suppose you weren't to get angry with her for looking down on you, how do you think you'd feel about you?

MRINMAYE SEN: At that moment, I was perfectly acceptable of myself. No problems.

WINDY: So you weren't viewing her looking down on you as a trigger that you would then look down on yourself?

MRINMAYE SEN: No.

[It is clear that my hypothesis is incorrect. Mrinmaye Sen's anger is not ego-defensive. As such, I let my hypothesis go.]

WINDY: So, what's anger-provoking about her looking down on you?

MRINMAYE SEN: … I know this one.

WINDY (said with humour): You know this one. It sounds like it's an old familiar one. It's the same old song.

MRINMAYE SEN: So, I expect that, when I have created and worked towards getting positive responses from people, I have established relationships where people are always going to comply with my request, people are always going to respect me, that's what I expect; that they are going to respect me all the time. Any single time that they don't, I am not yet willing to accept that.

WINDY: Yeah, exactly. So, you have a rule which says that if you give a good reason and a good rationale, that the other person, ideally, should respect you.

MRINMAYE SEN: Yes.

WINDY: Is that right?

MRINMAYE SEN: Yes.

WINDY: And that's important to you.

MRINMAYE SEN: Yes.

WINDY (sang with humour): R-E-S-P-E-C-T. Respect.

MRINMAYE SEN: Yes.

WINDY: We'll call you Aretha from now on[1] (said with humour). There's nothing wrong with that. Wanting to be respected, having respect from your boss, fine. When you don't get it, you're going to feel annoyed, disappointed, etc., but you felt angry, and we know that you felt angry for a day-and-a-half, ruminating, going over it, so we know that something else is going on. Let me review what we know and what we don't know. We know it's important to you to be respected, correct?

[I introduce the attitude assessment technique known as WRAP (see Chapter 2).]

MRINMAYE SEN: Yes.

WINDY: We know that, in this instance, you saw your boss's response to you as being disrespectful.

MRINMAYE SEN: Yes.

WINDY: Maybe even in the way that she did it as well, in that curt way was also a sign of disrespect, do you think?

MRINMAYE SEN: In the way?

WINDY: She was quite curt in the way she put things.

MRINMAYE SEN: Right.

WINDY: Did you see that as a sign of disrespect as well or is that a different issue?

MRINMAYE SEN: … No, actually I'm not getting your point.

WINDY: You said that there were two things that you were bothered about, stressed about: one is the fact that she said 'no' and you saw that as disrespect; and secondly you said that she responded to you in a curt manner.

MRINMAYE SEN: I think it's about the curt manner in which she responded to me. It's not just about she said no to my request.

WINDY: But you see that as a part of being disrespected.

MRINMAYE SEN: Slightly. Somewhat. That's not so much of a major issue. I can take no for an answer, but the very fact that she said that, 'When I said no, you need not ask me again.' I felt this curtness of her response; this was the most insulting part.

WINDY: OK, and that was the disrespecting part, was it?

MRINMAYE SEN: Yes. I felt that was disrespectful.

WINDY: OK. It's slightly different from what you said. You've moved the goalposts a little bit, but that's OK; we'll go along with this. So, what we know is that you like to be respected. You prefer to be respected.

[This interchange shows that it is important for the therapist in a VBTC to be open to changing their assessment at any time. Previously, I thought that there were two adversities – being disrespected by her boss and her boss's curt manner. In fact, the latter is a sign of the former and they are not separate.]

MRINMAYE SEN: True.

WINDY: You want a reasonable response, and, when you didn't get it, it would be regarded in your mind as disrespectful. We know that you prefer to be respected rather than disrespected, and we know that you took her response to you as evidence of disrespect. And we know that you were angry. You had the kind of anger that led you to be ruminating. We know that, OK?

[Having clarified the adversity at 'A' I continue with the WRAP technique introduced earlier to identify her rigid and alternative flexible attitudes.]

MRINMAYE SEN: Yes.

WINDY: We don't know what attitude that response was based on, so you can help me out here. So, Attitude 1 is: 'I prefer my boss to respect me, and, therefore, she has to.' Attitude 2 is: 'I prefer my boss to respect me, but, sadly and regretfully, she doesn't have to.' Now what accounts for your anger response that lasted for a day-and-a-half with extra rumination, the first or the second?

MRINMAYE SEN: The first one.

WINDY: How would you feel if you really believed the second, which is, 'I much prefer my boss to respect me, but, sadly and regretfully, she doesn't have to do so'? How would you feel if you got that into your belief system, your attitude system?

MRINMAYE SEN: Then I think I wouldn't be angry for so long.

WINDY: But you still wouldn't like it.

MRINMAYE SEN: I wouldn't like it, but then, if I really accept that, yeah, sadly, other people don't really have to respect me. They have their choice to not respect me.

WINDY: They do. They have a right to be wrong. So, let's then have a look. Which of those two attitudes do you think is more consistent with reality? 'Because I would prefer to be respected, therefore I have to be,' or, 'I want to be respected, but, sadly, I don't have to be, by my boss'? Which is more consistent with reality?

[I proceed to engage Mrinmaye Sen in a choice-based dialectical examination of her two opposing attitudes (see Chapter 2).]

MRINMAYE SEN: The second one.

WINDY: Which is healthier for you?

MRINMAYE SEN: The second one.

WINDY: Why?

MRINMAYE SEN: Because then I wouldn't be ruminating for a day-and-a-half's time.

WINDY: That's right.

MRINMAYE SEN: And I'd be working on everything else perfectly well.

WINDY: That's right, but you still would feel annoyed and healthily angry, because you prefer respect to disrespect, and that's important to you. So that's fine. Which seems to be more sensible of those two attitudes?

[Given that Mrinmaye Sen originally said that her goal was not to be bothered about being disrespected, I emphasise the constructiveness and realism of being annoyed and healthily angry and the adversity of disrespect.]

MRINMAYE SEN: The second one.

WINDY: Why?

MRINMAYE SEN: It is sensible because it is more of a logical thing.

WINDY: Yeah.

MRINMAYE SEN: It's more logical.

WINDY: It's recognising that there's no connection between what you want and what you have to get.

MRINMAYE SEN: Right.

WINDY: But there is a connection between what you want and the fact that you don't have to get it.

MRINMAYE SEN: Right.

WINDY: Now, when you look at giving up the rigid attitude and getting the flexible attitude – the rigid attitude is, 'My boss must respect me. I want her to and, therefore, she has to,' and the other one's saying, 'I want her to respect me, but, sadly, she doesn't have to' – do you feel any doubt or reservation about working towards giving up the rigid one and getting the flexible one? Do you want to keep the rigid one in some way? Do you have any attachment to it?

[As I discussed in Chapter 2, people can have doubts, reservations and objections (DROs) about developing their flexible / non-extreme attitudes and giving up their rigid / extreme attitudes and it is important to identify and deal with any that the volunteer has.]

MRINMAYE SEN: Well, the rigid one is the one that I've had for a long period of time, and it is the one that has helped me develop my personality, my ways of responding in such a way that I have experienced a lot of success with people.

WINDY: So, your rigid attitude has really helped you.

MRINMAYE SEN: Yes.

WINDY: I wonder. I wonder if it wasn't the preference that was part of your rigid attitude.

MRINMAYE SEN: A preference can be part of a rigid attitude as well?

WINDY: As I said, 'I want to be respected and, therefore, she has to.' That's a preference, isn't it?

MRINMAYE SEN: Mmm [yes].

WINDY: So, the preference is part of both the rigid attitude and the flexible attitude. My guess is that what's really helped you is the preference, not the rigidity, because normally rigidity helps a person to not make friends, to not be popular, to develop their personality in angry, black and white, rigid ways. But the flexibility helps you to be open. So, I would question that. But the other thing I think is right that, yes, this rigid attitude is like a comfortable pair of smelly, old slippers, and, when you get the new ones without the smell, which is the rigidity versus the flexibility, it's not going to be comfortable until you wear them in. What do you think you'd have to do to wear in these new attitudinal slippers of yours?

MRINMAYE SEN: Tolerate the shoe bite for some time.

WINDY: Tolerate that and practise it. But bear in mind that human beings ... are you human (said with humour)?

MRINMAYE SEN: Yes.

WINDY: Humans, in the heat of the moment, will go back to the more practised one. So, you'll start off by asking yourself unhealthily angry. Your job is to say, 'Aha, I know what I'm doing, I can run this programme, it's very familiar, I don't have to work at doing that, but I do have to work at going against that.' You're going to have to ask yourself, 'Am I prepared to tolerate the discomfort of working against that? And, if I do, I'll, quite quickly, show myself that she and other people don't have to respect me, even though that's what I want, and, given that, I may even have a discussion with her later.' That's another topic, but you do need to work at that. If you work at that, it will be interesting to find out what happens to you. But the initial response will be back to rigid, and that's why I always say the problem is not the first response, it's what you do then. Continuing it on that path, a nice familiar path, smelly slipperhood, or you go this way to the unfamiliar but healthy way of rational, flexible thinking. You're going to have to do that in a deliberate way. The more you do it, the more used to it you get. So, what do you reckon? Do you want to do that?

[If you recall, Mrinmaye Sen wanted to feel instantly unbothered about being disrespected. I dealt with the unrealism of the 'not bothered' goal and in the previous response, I spell out the likelihood that Mrinmaye Sen's first response to disrespect will be unhealthy anger. This is the case because it is based on rigid thinking which is the more rehearsed and familiar response. As such, it is to be expected and is not a problem unless she regards it as one. I point out that she can regard this first response as a cue for flexible thinking about the adversity.]

MRINMAYE SEN: Sure, I think I should try.
WINDY: I'm not asking you to try.

[It is important to distinguish between a commitment to try and a commitment to do. I routinely make this distinction when people say they will try to do something rather than they will do it.]

MRINMAYE SEN: I should definitely work on it and keep reminding myself that everybody has the right to not respect me, and I can be completely OK with that.
WINDY: I don't want you to be completely OK with it. I want you to be healthily un-OK with it.

[Again, I intervene to challenge Mrinmaye Sen's unrealistic goal of being 'completely OK' in response to disrespect and offer being healthily un-OK with it as a more realistic alternative.]

MRINMAYE SEN: Yeah, I can be healthily un-OK about it.
WINDY: Get it? Because 'OK' means it doesn't really matter; it's good. Unhealthily OK means, 'I'm going to be displeased about that because of my preference, but it's going to be healthy.' So, you go and work at that.

Follow-up: seven months later[2]

Prof. Dryden was lucid and helped understand the topic with greater understanding. I learned that confirming with the client exactly what disturbance to work on is of pivotal importance. I also learnt that when the subject is important for a person, things not happening according to his or her wish cannot lead to neutral feelings; one will always have a negative feeling about situations that are important and don't conform with the person's expectations. As therapists, we have to help the client understand that they can have a healthy negative emotion instead of an unhealthy negative emotion but again if the subject is important the client cannot feel neutral towards the subject.

I solved my problem after the one on one brief therapy with Prof. Dryden, and after a few months, I realised that such similar triggers were not bothering me as much. In fact, a few weeks back a similar trigger occurred, but I was able to get over the problem very quickly, seems like after disputing the basic irrational belief I had achieved deeper inside and internalise the new learning.

Now in my private practice, I encourage my clients not to hope for neutral feelings towards subjects of importance but work towards acceptance of healthy negative feelings.

Notes

1 This is a reference to a famous song by the soul singer, Aretha Franklin called 'Respect'.
2 See Appendix 2 for the email I sent to volunteers requesting a follow-up.

Chapter 11

Being envied and treated unfairly

Overview

In this VBTC lasting 16 minutes 16 seconds, Prats discusses with me her problems when people envy her and treat her unfairly. In both situations she feels hurt and does not respond to the other person. Thus, as Paul Hauck, the well-known REBT therapist, was fond of saying she gets from others the behaviour that she is prepared to put up with without protest (Hauck, 1991). In this interview, I help Prats to identify and respond to her rigid attitude that others must not treat her in the way that she does not deserve. In developing her alternative flexible attitude, Prats incorrectly thinks that this attitude would lead her not to be bothered about being treated unfairly (a recurring theme in the interviews presented in this book). Rather, it would lead her to feel healthily sad or disappointed about the adversity. I also help Prats to develop a way of asserting herself with the other based on REBT principles.

The VBTC

WINDY: OK, Prats, how can I help you today?

PRATS: ... I am staying in Muscat now with my husband, in Oman. Now it will be five years that I am married, so, after marriage, life has been pretty good. Although mine is an arranged marriage, I don't feel like it's an arranged marriage, and it was basically my choice that I want to do an arranged marriage. Before marriage, I had dated guys, but, after dating, I felt that an arranged marriage was the best option. So, then everything is going fine with my husband and me, but, in Muscat, we have a group of friends, and they keep taunting. They keep saying things which I feel hurt about, like they will say, 'Your husband spends so much for you,' or something like that, which I get really hurt about. An example of that will be, before coming to India from Muscat, one of my friends said, 'You are spending so much on your daughter, and I hope that you can afford to do that in the future.' I felt a little hurt. I did not say anything to her, but then I felt hurt about why does she have to comment on what I'm doing for my daughter, or something like that. So, I just feel that I just ignore such comments and I don't say anything blankly to them. I'm just thinking that I should just comment and be forward and open.

WINDY: And what would you say?

PRATS: I think I should have said, 'It is my personal life, and, if me and my husband are OK with it, if we can afford something, it's not something for you to worry about.'

WINDY: And what would your prediction be if you had said that?

PRATS: I think she would have kept quiet and she would have not passed on comments.

WINDY: And what did you say to these other people who taunted you with your financial situation?

PRATS: I just keep quiet. I ignore it.

WINDY: And what happens?

PRATS: Nothing. Then they keep saying it again.

WINDY: So, could it be the fact you don't say anything is linked to the possibility that they may keep saying things?

[Very often, people take an individual's silence to mean assent.]

PRATS: Yes, I think I'm giving them a hand that they can just say anything and they can get away with it.

WINDY: Yeah, as I said the other day, Paul Hauck said, 'You get the behaviour from other people that you're prepared to put up with, without protest.'

PRATS: Yes.

WINDY: How would you feel about nicely pointing out that, 'Don't worry about it, I'm OK,' and come up with some response to indicate that you don't welcome such comments? What do you think would, first of all, happen if you did that?

PRATS: Yeah.

WINDY: What's your prediction about what would happen?

PRATS: I think they might talk behind my back.

WINDY: Do they have a right to do that?

PRATS: Yes, they do.

WINDY (said with humour): OK, exactly. I'm pretty sure people taunt me behind my back. I'm going to go through the world stopping them! Wait a minute, they're taunting me behind my back in Russia – right, I'm off! So, you're only concerned about them taunting you in front of your back ... or in front of you. Are you stopping yourself from speaking up in some way?

PRATS: I am stopping myself in speaking out to them because I feel you speak out when you believe that change might take place in a person.

WINDY: So, you want a guarantee first, and then you'll speak up?

PRATS: Yeah.

WINDY: You want a guarantee?

PRATS: Yeah, I was looking for a guarantee.

WINDY (said with humour): Well, you can look. There's nothing wrong with looking. I believe one was last seen flying over the Indian Ocean towards God knows where. What's my point?

PRATS: I think I should be open and vocal in a firm and assertive way; that I'm not liking such comments.

WINDY: The point is you like to have a guarantee, and that's understandable, but your choices are to either hold the attitude, 'I'd like to have a guarantee, but I don't need it, ...'

PRATS: I don't need it.

WINDY: ... or, 'I'd like to have a guarantee, and I need it, and I'm not going to act until I get it.'

PRATS: No, I think I shall act without a guarantee.

WINDY: Yeah, OK. Anything else stopping you?

PRATS: No, that's it. I also feel sometimes that I might hurt the person.

WINDY: Hurt the person?

PRATS: Yeah, maybe they might not take it well.

WINDY: OK, let's see, let's judge. Imagine that I've just made a comment about your financial situation, it may even be based on envy, I don't know.

PRATS: It is mostly envy, actually, yeah. I can get that.

WINDY: Exactly, OK. So, I've made a comment, and your task is to give me a response to indicate that you're not quite happy with that and you'd rather not hear it. So, let me hear what you say, and then we can judge how likely that is going to be hurtful. So, for example, if I were to say to you, 'Shut up and don't say these things because if you do, I'll smash you in the face!' it's probably going to hurt the person (said with humour).

PRATS: Yeah.

WINDY: So let's see how you would do it.

PRATS: OK. ... I will say, ... 'OK, you have commented, but then I don't like you commenting again and again on my financial status, because whatever I have, it's not my choice. It's not in anyone's control to be in a particular financial status. So why are you telling me something? It is by God's grace that we are doing well, and I cannot predict about the future what it is going to be for my child, but definitely I don't want to think about it from now.'

WINDY: OK. So, having heard yourself, how much potential hurt is there in that statement?

PRATS: I don't think there is any.

WINDY: No. Can I model an alternative for you?

PRATS: Yes.

WINDY: Then we can compare the two. So, you've just said something, and I'd say something like, 'I understand what you've said, but I actually would prefer that you didn't make a comment on my financial status. You have a right to say anything, but I would prefer it if you didn't, because I don't find it very helpful in our relationship. Can we agree on that?' or something like that.

[In modelling assertion for Prats, I have included a flexible attitude about the person making comments on Prats' financial situation and the offer of an agreed way forward. This is characteristic of an REBT approach to assertion.]

PRATS: Yeah.

WINDY: So, if you really show yourself, it would be nice to know for sure what's going to happen and that they're not going to be hurt, but you don't need that.

PRATS: Yes.

WINDY: But let's suppose you say it in the most gentle way and she feels hurt. Let's just suppose that, because that could happen.

PRATS: That could happen, yes.

WINDY: How would you feel about her feelings of hurt?

PRATS: I will feel sorry that she's hurt, but then, obviously, she should also understand that I also felt the same when she did it to me.

WINDY: So that wouldn't stop you from doing it again?

PRATS: Yeah.

WINDY: So, you'd just feel sorry for her.

PRATS: Yes.

[I am checking to see if Prats would have a behaviour-inhibiting emotional problem about the other person feeling hurt and her response indicates that she hasn't.]

WINDY: OK, alright, that sounds quite reasonable. Anything else you want to bring up about this?

PRATS: Yeah, just, with regards to the same person, there was an incident where I had posted a comment on Facebook, and this lady openly went ahead and commented something against me and also against one of my friends, who is very senior to me, I would say; who is very expert with children. If I have any issues with children, I will go to that lady and consult her. So, she said something against that lady and me, which was not at all related to her.

WINDY: Right, and how did you feel?

PRATS: I was shocked, looking at such a comment on Facebook, and the topic was not related; why is she saying such things on social media? I just deleted all the comments because I did not want to get into the mud fight.

WINDY: Right, but how did you feel?

PRATS: I was very hurt.

WINDY: OK, so you've mentioned hurt a couple of times, so let's focus on hurt.

[Rather than make a unilateral decision to focus on hurt, it would have been better for me to invite Prats to make this the focus of our conversation at this point.]

PRATS: Yeah.

WINDY: Shall we focus on hurt on this episode or the first episode that you worked on?

PRATS: This episode.

WINDY: OK, so what were you hurt about?

PRATS: I was hurt because I never say anything to anyone. I am the kind of person who will not interfere. I am least bothered about what is going on in others' lives. When she commented in such a way, and she is a lawyer and a blogger, so she always expects and feels that, if I like her blogs or if I recommend her blogs to someone, she'll get more likes. She has that, but I'm always ignoring and I'm not liking her blogs because, somehow, I don't like it, and I'm ignoring it.

WINDY: And she might not like that.

PRATS: Yeah, I think she knows that I don't.

WINDY: And she notices that you ignore her.

PRATS: Yes.

WINDY: OK, so that might explain why she's done that. But do you think you deserve this or not?

PRATS: I do not deserve it.

[While I could have been more explicit about my AC assessment of this episode where 'C' = hurt and 'A' = the woman, in question, treating Prats in a way that she thinks she did not deserve. My sense, at the time, was that Prats understood this. Nevertheless, it is best to be explicit in a VBTC assessment.]

WINDY: No, OK. Let me ask you a question: are you ready for the cod liver oil (said with humour)?

PRATS: Yes.

WINDY: Are you ready (said with humour)?

PRATS: Yes.

WINDY: Are you sure (said with humour)?

PRATS: Yes.

WINDY: Here we go, let me ask you a question: you don't deserve it, right?

PRATS: Yeah.

WINDY: Why do you have to get what you deserve?

[Again, I am skipping over a few steps in this dialectical examination. It would have been better for me to establish that Prats agreed that she held a rigid attitude towards the adversity before I helped her to examine it.]

PRATS: Yeah, I don't.

WINDY: You don't?

PRATS: Yes.

WINDY: Now, if you really believed that, how would you feel about what she did?

PRATS: I will not be bothered.

WINDY: Yes, you would.

PRATS: Yeah.

WINDY: You would be bothered.

PRATS: Yeah.

WINDY: And you should be bothered.

PRATS: Yes.

WINDY: Do you know why? Why?

PRATS: Because she has made a threat to me by commenting.

WINDY: And your preference is what?

PRATS: To be less concerned, maybe.

WINDY: No, your preference about her behaviour.

PRATS: That she should not cross the boundaries.

WINDY: Preferably.

PRATS: Preferably.

WINDY: OK, so your preference is, 'I'd prefer her not to cross a boundary, partly because I haven't done anything to deserve it, however, I don't have to get what I deserve. But, as I prefer her not to do that, I'm sad or I'm disappointed,' or whatever it is, 'that it's happened.' So, don't try to persuade yourself it doesn't matter, because it does.

[While REBT outlines a sequence in assessment and intervention (see Chapter 2), it is important that the therapist is flexible while using this sequence in working with a given client or volunteer. Thus, here, in responding to the unrealistic nature of Prats' statement that she would not be bothered if she did not hold a rigid attitude to the woman's behaviour, I show her that she would feel a healthy negative emotion such as sadness or disappointment because she would hold a flexible attitude which I then spell out for her. Here, I am making the 'B-C' between the flexible basic attitude at 'B' and the healthy response at 'C' in reaction to what is being discussed in the VBTC even though it is out of sequence.]

PRATS: Yes.

WINDY: So that's the cod liver oil moment, to recognise that, just because you don't deserve it, doesn't mean that it mustn't happen to you.

PRATS: Yes.

WINDY: And I think the reason why it is happening to you is that she is guided, not by your deservingness, but by your lack of liking on Facebook (said with humour).

PRATS: Yes, and, in fact, after this Facebook incident, she still has the courage, she's sending me private messages to like her blogs again, and I'm continuously ignoring it.

WINDY: Yeah.

PRATS: But I think now I should tell her. After going back to Muscat, I'll just have a talk with her.

WINDY: Have a talk with her in the same way, because there is a relationship between hurt and not saying anything.

[Here, I point out to Prats that hurt is associated with not communicating to the other person.]

PRATS: Yes, not saying anything. Exactly.

WINDY: And the more you don't say anything, the more people think you're OK with it, or they don't know that you're not OK with it, and the more they do it, and, the more they do it, the more you feel hurt, and then you don't say anything.

PRATS: Yeah.

WINDY: So, if you can, 1) show yourself that, sadly, you don't have to get what you want, just because you don't deserve it, it doesn't mean it mustn't happen to you; 2) to recognise that you don't need a guarantee as to how things are going to come across; and here's my additional for you to think about – what I want you to think about is your tolerance level for interpersonal unease / conflict, because I'm hearing that you like things smooth.

PRATS: Yes.

WINDY: If you like things smooth, hang out in a mortuary with dead people, because live people, they've got a mind of their own (said with humour). So that's what I want you to think about.

[I want to make two points here. First, it may have been better for me to ask Prats to summarise and for me to fill in the blanks. Second, note at the end I make explicit the issue of her preference for interpersonal smoothness. While I think that she holds a demand about this at the point of assertion, I wonder whether it was wise for me to bring the subject up as a topic for her to think about or would it have been better to say nothing given that I did not have the time to help Prats to deal with

it if it was a problem for her? However, because she has the option to request the recording and transcript of the session which she can review and think about, I decided to introduce this new topic at the end.]

Follow-up: seven months later[1]

My experience of the interview: it was an eye-opening session for me. In the session, I realised that I always kept quiet and didn't express my opinions when someone said something to me. I was giving an impression to others that they can say anything to me and I would be relaxed about me.

- *I learned in the session the art of expressing my thoughts and opinions to the other person without hurting them. Earlier I used to think that by expressing my opinions I would hurt the other person but it is after the session I realised that by not expressing my thoughts and opinions I might actually be sending the wrong message across to the other person involved.*
- *I have solved my issues to a great extent after the session. I am at peace, and I definitely can't control how others think about me, but I can definitely control my reaction to the problem.*
- *Now I know how important it is to solve the problem at the right time and to address the issue there itself rather than delaying it.*
- *I am using this principle in dealing with all my issues after that session.*
- *Professor Dryden played a very important role in making me realise that I can't control the way others think and I can't make everyone happy.*
- *I did request the recording and transcript of the session, and it's been useful introspection and for dealing with other cases.*

Note

1   See Appendix 2 for the email I sent to volunteers requesting a follow-up.

Chapter 12

Dog phobia

Overview

In this VBTC lasting 16 minutes and 14 seconds, Ananya discusses her dog phobia with me. The reason that she still has this problem is that she has not faced dogs repeatedly until she is no longer afraid of them. In the course of the interview, I explain the importance of a) tolerating her initial fear, b) having a plan to seek medical help in case a dog does bite her and c) understanding that her thoughts 'I'll die' stem from the rigid and extreme attitudes she holds towards her fear and the prospect of being bitten and that these thoughts are much less likely to be produced when her attitudes are flexible and non-extreme. At the end of the interview, Ananya resolves to go running regularly where she may encounter dogs while implementing the above.

The VBTC

WINDY: OK, Ananya, what problem can I help you with?

ANANYA: So, this was an issue that I had brought up even in January – I wanted to work on my fear of dogs.

WINDY: Fear of dogs?

ANANYA: Yes. So, what happened at that time was we, as in my husband and I, were planning to buy a dog, so I was working on the fear, and I was pretty comfortable at one point, when a dog came really close to me. I would feel a little uncomfortable, but I was OK with the dog being around. Then, eventually, we decided not to have the dog because of all practical reasons; we decided not to buy a dog. Then the fear, somehow, came back. And what is happening right now is I'm training for the half marathon and I would like to go for my runs early in the morning, and that's the time when there are street dogs all over the place. So I will see that. And what happened a couple of days ago is that, when I was walking on the road, I was walking not even running, and a dog jumped at me from behind. It was playful, apparently, because apparently it was all happy and running around, and it jumped at me for some reason, and then the fear has come back.

WINDY: How did you know it was friendly and happy?

ANANYA: Because there were other people who were really happy with it being there, so I'm guessing it was. It was wagging its tail and playing with them, and maybe it thought I wanted to play with it too, but I didn't want to.

WINDY: No, OK. So, you said that you brought this up in January?

ANANYA: Yes.

WINDY: What do you mean by that?

ANANYA: During my primary and advanced.

WINDY: You mean in peer counselling?

ANANYA: In peer counselling[1], yes.

WINDY: OK, right, OK. And, as a result of that, you decided to get a dog or what?

ANANYA: No. So, we eventually decided to get a dog. It wasn't because of the peer counselling. But then, actually, that, as a goal, was motivating enough for me to work on the anxiety. I would actually call it anxiety because, when I see dogs from a distance, I start trying to think, 'What do I do? Do I cross the road? OK, maybe I should start walking,' and that's affecting my pace, because I'm trying to get better with my pace. So right now it's coming in the way of my training.

WINDY: OK. So, what do you think would've happened if you were still going to get a dog and you still had that experience that you mentioned about the dog that jumped up at you? What do you think would've happened?

ANANYA: I don't know whether I would've still freaked out or whether I would've been OK, because I think somewhere I kept telling myself that this is going to be normal; it's going to be part of my home.

WINDY: 'And since it's going to be part of my home,' what?

ANANYA: I would be OK with it being around, maybe even like it being around.

WINDY: And that would've been the case even if the dog jumped up at you?

ANANYA: I would maybe be happy should it do it or maybe think in mind that it would be OK. I think so. I don't know.

WINDY: So, even if you had the same experience, if you had decided to get a dog, you would've what?

ANANYA: Maybe I would've told myself that, when I get a dog, it will also jump at me, so maybe it's not such a scary thing.

WINDY: Right, OK. So ... how about if you had the dog and then this dog jumped up at you, would you get rid of the dog that you had?

ANANYA: No.

WINDY: Why not?

ANANYA: Because by then it would be part of our family.

WINDY: Yeah, OK, and therefore not a dog to be scared of?

ANANYA: Yes.

WINDY: Even though it might jump up at you?

ANANYA: Yes.

WINDY: OK.

ANANYA: And also I think somewhere I would think that my husband would be around, initially. My husband loves dogs, so maybe that was also comforting for me. I'm just thinking out loud now.

WINDY: Does your husband work?

ANANYA: Yes.

WINDY: Do you work?

ANANYA: Yes.

WINDY: Do you work full time?

ANANYA: Yes.

WINDY: And are there times when your husband is not there?

ANANYA: Isn't around, yes.

WINDY: So, he wouldn't be around to protect you?

ANANYA: Right.

WINDY: And then what?

ANANYA: Right.

WINDY: You would be around to protect yourself.

ANANYA: Right.

WINDY: OK. How would you do that?

ANANYA: Like I said, I think I would think that, now that we've got the dog, it's our conscious decision to.

WINDY: OK. 'I've made a conscious decision and I've made friends with the dog.'

ANANYA: Yeah.

WINDY: Right, OK. So how do you view the dog that jumped up at you?

ANANYA: Evil.

WINDY: Evil? OK, right.

ANANYA: Yeah, like later on.

WINDY: We're going to have to give you unconditional dog-acceptance.

[A humorous riff on the REBT concept of unconditional other-acceptance.]

ANANYA: Yeah.

WINDY: You mean that was your initial reaction or is that your considered reaction?

ANANYA: Honestly speaking, when the dog came running, like I said it was playing around, and I was contemplating the idea of crossing the road at that time, but, for some reason, I didn't, and then it went behind and then it jumped at me. So, I was thinking, at that time, I said, 'Oh God, I should've just crossed the road.' But then I understand that that's not a way out.

WINDY: Not if you want to overcome your fear.

ANANYA: Yes.

WINDY: That's correct. So, after the dog jumped up at you, what happened?

ANANYA: So my heartbeat went fast, and it licked me also. So, it licked my hand.

WINDY (said with humour): Do dogs do that?

ANANYA: They don't do that to me usually.

WINDY (said with humour): No, they've got a special dispensation for that.

ANANYA: But then I tried to tell myself that, that, 'You're actually scared, and this dog jumped up at you and it actually licked you, and you have still survived.' So, I tried doing that, but, somehow, I don't know, it didn't work for me.

WINDY: Well, what didn't work for you?

ANANYA: I was thinking that, if I keep saying that to myself, later, when I see another dog, I won't cross the road, but I still did.

WINDY: OK. But the point is, when the dog jumped up at you and licked you, were you anxious at that point?

ANANYA: I didn't know that it would, so when I realised it, yes, I screamed out loud.

WINDY: And then what happened?

ANANYA: And then, after some time, I got OK.

WINDY: OK, you got OK?

ANANYA: Yes.

WINDY: How long after that?

ANANYA: 30 seconds.

WINDY: 30 seconds? OK, so you had a fear reaction, right, and then, after 30 seconds, it went down.

ANANYA: Yes.

WINDY: OK. You see, two things occur to me. It would be interesting to hear what your feedback is. One is that you're not seeing these dogs as a dog that you haven't made friends with yet; you see this as evil or whatever, but then, when you think, 'Well, I can make friends with a dog, potentially, and, when I do, I'll be alright with it.' And the other thing that occurs to me is that you have an experience where you have 30 seconds of fear and then it goes down.

ANANYA: Yeah.

[Whatever we talk about, if Ananya wants to tackle her fear of dogs effectively she needs to face them in reality rather than avoid them. What I do from this point in the interview is to help her to see that she can tolerate her initial feelings of fear and to come up with a plan if a dog bites her.]

WINDY: So I'm wondering if, first of all, what would happen if you allowed yourself to see the dog as somebody that you haven't yet made friends with. You may not, but, if you did, you'd be able to get on with it, and what would happen if you allowed yourself, but to not like, the idea that you might get anxious for 30 seconds and then it will go down?

ANANYA: But I think what comes to my mind for the second bit that you mentioned is that this time maybe I was lucky, but what if I got bitten?

WINDY: Well, what if you got bitten? What if you did?

ANANYA: I would've had to take those injections.

WINDY: Correct, yeah.

ANANYA: And it might be an injury that would take time to heal.

WINDY: It might, yeah.

ANANYA: Yeah.

WINDY: And?

ANANYA: That wouldn't be a good feeling.

WINDY: No, it wouldn't be a good feeling.

ANANYA: Very painful.

WINDY: Painful, yeah. The bite or the injection?

ANANYA: Both.

WINDY: Both, OK. Alright, so you'll have some pain, and then what?

ANANYA: And then, after some time, I would heal.

WINDY: That's right. Now, if you say that to yourself, remind yourself, 'Well, look, even if I got bitten, that would be a pain in the arse, it would be painful, but I'd go to wherever you go to get injected and things like that,' because, at the moment, what do you think you're saying about the prospect of getting bitten and all the pain?

ANANYA: Yeah, I think, in my head, I'm thinking I will die.

WINDY: 'I'll die,' from what? The bite or the injection or the what?

ANANYA: Or the fear, or the combination of everything.

WINDY: Right. Do you think that happens because you're saying, 'Well, look, I don't like the instant anxiety, it's a pain in the arse, I don't have to be free of it,' or do you think you're saying, 'Oh my God, I mustn't be anxious around dogs'?

[The REBT explanation of highly distorted thoughts like 'I'll die' in this context is that they stem from rigid and extreme attitudes rather than from flexible and non-extreme attitudes (see Chapter 1). In the following exchanges, I help Ananya to see this.]

ANANYA: Sorry, I didn't understand the second bit that you said.

WINDY: Do you think you're saying, 'I prefer not to be anxious around dogs, but that doesn't mean I mustn't. It's a pain in the arse if I was,' or do you think your attitude is, 'I mustn't be anxious'?

ANANYA: I mustn't be anxious.

WINDY: And, when you hold the attitude, 'I mustn't be anxious about dogs,' does that lead or not lead to the idea that you're going to die?

ANANYA: It leads to it.

WINDY: That's right. So what would you believe if you really show yourself, 'Look, it'll be a pain in the arse if I get anxious, it'll be a pain in the arse if I get bitten on the arse,' because it would be a pain in the arse if you got bitten on the arse (said with humour) 'and it would be a pain in the arm if I got injected, but I can allow these things to happen and they don't have to not happen'? What would happen to the idea that you're going to die?

ANANYA: ... It wouldn't feature anywhere.

WINDY: That's right. So, you see, what you're doing is you seem to be avoiding your own creation of, 'I'm going to die,' because of your intolerance of your fear and the pain. And, of course, you've got a very easy alternative – cross over the road. Let me tell you what happened to me. I was bitten by an Alsatian dog, and it wasn't very playful at the time, and I was 7 years old. I did actually develop a fear of big dogs. Actually, probably all dogs. So, I did, literally, cross over the road. And then I learnt about REBT and I decided to do something about it, and, actually, even though part of me was saying, 'Cross over the road,' the other part of me was saying, 'Actually approach the dog,' and I decided to actually approach dogs rather than let the dogs approach me. I don't know whether the dogs were scared of me or not (said with humour). I approached dogs because I saw that that was the best way of dealing with it, and I allowed myself to be fearful. Now the result of that is that I still get a twinge of fear sometimes, sometimes I don't, and I just accept it. Now what lesson do you think my experience has got for you?

[Therapist self-disclosure can be a highly effective technique in helping volunteers understand the nature of their problem and what can be done about it. It is usual for the therapist to ask the volunteer for permission to self-disclose and I wished I had done so.]

ANANYA: ... Firstly, it's OK to be fearful.

WINDY: That's right.

ANANYA: And, second, that whether or not I face the dogs, the fear is going to exist.

WINDY: Right.

ANANYA: I'd much rather face the dogs and then experience the fear, rather than cross over and still experience the fear.

WINDY: Right. And, actually, you can make friends with the dog. I don't know what street dogs are like in India. What are they like in general, if we're going to appeal to your non-phobic part of you? Objectively, what are they like?

ANANYA: Honestly speaking, the place where I live, Amila Rd., there are too many constructions taking place, and there are at least ten dogs in every construction site. So it's like a warzone all the time for them. There's one group barking at the other group, and, as a result, what happens is anyone who goes past or whether there's a bike or a car or whether there's someone on the bicycle, the dogs are barking at them too, sometimes running behind them.

[If I had known this earlier, I may not have spent time on the 'make friends with the dog' strategy.]

WINDY: Sure.

ANANYA: So, when I witness these things, I'm like, 'OK, I'm going to go running there,' the very thought, then I start strategising in terms of maybe I should not take this route.

WINDY: OK, but what happens if you decide to say, 'Look, I'm going to go running. I would prefer a dog not to bark at me, but I'm going to allow a dog to bark at me. I'm going to allow myself to initially be fearful, but I'm going to run even though I might get afraid and even though the dog may bark at me,' what do you think would happen then?

ANANYA: I think I'm not OK to say to myself that I'm ready to allow the dog to bite me.

WINDY: Bark at you.

ANANYA: Bark at you, yeah.

WINDY (said with humour): I'm not suggesting, 'OK, let them bite me. Come on, bite me. Put a nice bit of meat paste on my arm. Have a go at that.' No, not even I would do that. But, if it does bite you, you've got a plan. What's the plan again?

ANANYA: I don't know.

WINDY: You told it.

ANANYA: ... I told you that I have a plan?

WINDY: If you got bitten.

ANANYA: I will just go and get the injections done. I don't know.

WINDY: That's the plan. No?

ANANYA: Yeah.

WINDY: You get the wound healed and the injection done, should it come to that, OK?

ANANYA: Yeah.

WINDY: So, let me ask you the question again: what would happen if you ran and you allowed the dogs to bark, and you didn't like it, but you allowed them to, and you allowed yourself to be fearful initially? What do you think would happen after a while?

ANANYA: I would've continued ... with my run. So, two things: one, my pace wouldn't be affected, and, second, I would feel happy that I didn't get affected by the dogs.

WINDY: And, if you did this every day, you practised that philosophy and running every day, what do you think would happen after a while?

ANANYA: I wouldn't be bothered by the dogs barking anymore. It would be part of the noise.

WINDY: You still may not like it. So that's the way to overcome your fear, you see, by allowing yourself but not liking the fact that you'll initially become scared, by allowing the dogs to bark even though it's unpleasant, to have a plan in case you're bitten, and to roll this out repeatedly. Will you do that?

ANANYA: Yes, I will.

WINDY: Good. OK. Well, that's very good to know.

[Ananya commits herself to the plan of running regularly, tolerating the fear and seeking medical help for any dog bites that she might receive.]

Follow-up: seven months later[2]

Thank you very much for being my therapist and helping me understand the various aspects of my fear of dogs. Some of the things that really worked for me, both while the session was being conducted and at an after-thought level, was the understanding of the secondary emotional problem, i.e. the anxiety about my anxiety. This was something that I was able to put into practice almost immediately, from the next day onwards, where I allowed myself to feel anxious whenever I saw dogs in the vicinity. And this helped me calm down to quite an extent.

What I liked most about the interview was that the assessment evaluated and addressed all the irrational beliefs, and also the secondary emotional problem. In addition, it also gave me an insight into how I actually have a plan of action, in case I got bitten by dogs. The latter, however, still does make me a bit wary whenever I think about it, but the level of anxiety is not how it used to be. The recording of the session was very helpful because I would play it and listen to it often, especially before going for my run, and that helped me focus on my run to a great extent.

I would like to cite one incident that took place after my session with Prof. Dryden. I was out for a picnic with my friends at a resort. Being an early riser, I decided to go for a run. As soon as I went a few metres away from my room, a dog came running towards me suspiciously, barking loudly. About four dogs followed it, and I was circled by them, was being barked at, and jumped at by one of them. It made me feel really uncomfortable and scared, and I just kept repeating to myself that it is okay to feel anxious, and I will soon be okay. I stood there, and the dogs eventually stopped barking. What I didn't know, however, is how to move away, because I kept standing there and the dogs kept standing there too. I called out for help, and a person from housekeeping came to my rescue. I think I did a pretty good job at managing myself, because I continued to go for my run afterwards, and didn't give up.

About Prof. Dryden, it was amazing how he built the therapeutic alliance so quickly and beautifully. His ability to use humour also made my session a lot of fun, and it helped me look at my problem from a different perspective. Most importantly, in the short duration of twenty odd minutes, he managed to make me realise my demands, my awfulising beliefs as well as my secondary emotional problem, and that was truly amazing!

As for my problem, it still exists, and I am still not too comfortable at the idea of going running in areas where dogs bark all the time, but I have managed to convince myself to face the fear rather than avoid the situation.

Thanks a lot for the session!

Notes

1   As part of initial training courses in REBT, participants have to counsel one another to practise the development of their REBT skills.
2   See Appendix 2 for the email I sent to volunteers requesting a follow-up.

Chapter 13

Physical pain

Overview

In this VBTC lasting 17 minutes and 3 seconds, Anahita discusses her anxiety problem relating to her physical back pain. Her anxiety stems from the rigid attitude that if she does all the right things with respect to her back then she has to have a guarantee that she will be able to control her pain as a result. Given that such a guarantee does not exist, the only thing her rigid attitude creates is anxiety and, in particular, the image that she has of herself as being bedridden. I help Anahita see not only the connection between this image and her rigid attitude but also the connection between her flexible attitude and the alternative image of her doing the best that she can under difficult circumstances. In addition, her flexible attitude would help her to feel in greater emotional control in the face of uncertainty.

The VBTC

WINDY: OK, Anahita, how can I help you today? What problem would you like help with?

ANAHITA: I've been having back pain on and off. About a year ago the pain activated to a level that it was about a nine on a ten. I met up with doctors and, for about seven months there was a misdiagnosis; I was on the wrong kinds of drugs. Subsequently, I have been on treatment and things are under control. So, the medicines are working; I just need to be on the meds all the time, which is fine, I've reconciled to that, and exercise. I have a tendency to awfulise and be very anxious about the pain and things, but now I genuinely do have a problem on an off day.

WINDY: On an off day?

ANAHITA: On a day when the pain is not under control and it is probably, maybe at a four or a five, which is much less than earlier, but
still it is acute enough to get in the way of normal functioning.
So those are the bad days.

WINDY: So the bad days are that you have a four and a five.

ANAHITA: Right.

WINDY: And why is that a bad day?

ANAHITA: A four on a ten, actually.

WINDY: No, four or five out of ten.

ANAHITA: Out of ten, yes.

WINDY: Yeah. And because normally it would be what these days?

ANAHITA: It would be at a two with the medication and the exercise.

WINDY: Right, so you've gone from a nine out of ten to ...

ANAHITA: Yes, to a two or a three out of ten. So, the pain is constant,
but it's well under control and it doesn't get in the way.

WINDY: But, occasionally, even though you're still on the medication,
it goes up to a five.

ANAHITA: Yes, up to a five.

WINDY: So that's a bad pain day.

ANAHITA: That's a bad pain day.

WINDY: Right.

ANAHITA: And I feel a little out of control because it's completely
unpredictable; I don't know when that happens, even if my
habits stay regular and consistent. So, I'm doing pretty much
the same kind of thing for a week. For example, for the past few
days I've been almost pain free, but then I never know when the
tide will turn and pain might aggravate. So, it just catches me off
guard and I don't feel good on those days.

WINDY: So, you can't predict. You can't make predictions.

ANAHITA: I can't make predictions.

WINDY: Or, if you can, sometimes the predictions don't come true.

ANAHITA: I don't try to predict.

WINDY: OK, no. So, what happens is that sometimes, for no apparent
reason, it sounds like – is that correct? – that the pain might go
up to a five?

ANAHITA: Right.

WINDY: And that is what you would call a bad pain day.

ANAHITA: Right.

WINDY: So, do you have an emotional problem about this?

ANAHITA: Yes. So, I get a little teary-eyed at that time for a while. I feel a loss of control. I feel it's not OK for it to be surfacing now and again in this manner.

WINDY: True, it's not OK.

ANAHITA: Yeah, it's not OK.

WINDY: Because what's your preference?

ANAHITA: That ... there'd be some consistency. I mean I'm looking at an 'A' that would be under control. If pain can be moderate or if I could know that particular things aggravate the pain, that would really help.

WINDY: Yeah, well, and that may be an ongoing process, but it sounds like, as part of that process, sometimes you say that you feel out of control.

[So far, Anahita has referred to common adversities in anxiety – uncertainty / unpredictability and lack of control.]

ANAHITA: Yeah.

WINDY: Now what emotion do you experience when you, using your language, 'feel out of control'?

ANAHITA: I think it's a mix of anxiety and ... extreme sadness. Very, very sad and anxiety, I think. A lot of anxiety.

WINDY: So, what would you like me to help you with? The anxiety?

ANAHITA: Well, if things are like this when I'm nearing 60, imagine what's going to happen down the road. Even if I'm doing things that are under my control, still some things, like pain, are not completely under my control as such. So, with age and degeneration, what else is going to happen? There has been a lot of ill health in the family; my parents, I've seen them go through long periods of very bad health.

WINDY: So, at the moment, you're thinking about a process of sort of degeneration as you get older.

ANAHITA: Yeah.

WINDY: And your preference there is what?

ANAHITA: That, even if that happens, that pain remains moderate. It's almost like I'm saying that, if I'm doing everything that I can, shouldn't all this just be better?

WINDY: Right, OK. And so, when you say that, do you think you're treating yourself as a human or a robot?

ANAHITA: … [Pause] Isn't it fair to expect that I put in x amount of effort and I expect y kind of outcome?

WINDY: Isn't it fair? I don't know. Is it fair?

ANAHITA: Isn't it? Is it unfair on my part to say that or to ask myself that, if I'm complying with medication, doing my exercises and not doing anything silly to aggravate pain, then …

WINDY: OK. So, I'm hearing two things. You tell me what you're saying. The fair bit is that, 'When I do my exercises and when I do all the right things, therefore the fair bit is that I increase my chances of controlling my pain,' versus, 'If I do all these things, then, really, the fair thing is to have a guarantee.' So, which one are you operating on?

ANAHITA: Probably the second one.

WINDY: The guarantee?

ANAHITA: The guarantee, yeah.

WINDY: OK. Well, it would be nice to have a guarantee, but is it just nice and you need it or is it nice and you don't need it?

ANAHITA: Right now, I'm functioning from high need.

[I have helped Anahita to acknowledge that she has a preference: if she does all the right things then it would be nice to have a guarantee that she can control her pain. The trouble for Anahita is then she makes this preference rigid. In her words, she is functioning from high need.]

WINDY: High need?

ANAHITA: Yeah.

WINDY: OK. So, what would happen if you function from no need but high desire? 'I really would like to have a guarantee if I do all the right things I will be pain free, but, sadly and regretfully, given the fact that I'm human, it doesn't have to be that way, even though I'd really like it.'

ANAHITA: Yeah. Very sensible, but …

WINDY: Very sensible, but … (said with humour)?

ANAHITA: Yes.

WINDY: What's the 'but'?

ANAHITA: The 'but' is that then I have a visual picture of me bed-ridden, achy back.

[When a person holds a rigid attitude towards an adversity, then, as I discussed in Chapter 1, they will experience an unhealthy negative

emotion and will act or feel like acting in unconstructive ways. These
are the emotional and behavioural consequences of the rigid attitude.
In addition, as also discussed in Chapter 1, the person will also have a
variety of cognitive consequences of the rigid attitude which are highly
distorted and skewed to the negative. These cognitions can be in words
or images. Thus, when Anahita says that she has a picture of herself
bedridden with an achy back, my conceptualisation is that this is a cog-
nitive consequence of her previously expressed rigid attitude. I set out
to help her to understand this by using a variant of the WRAP tech-
nique discussed in Chapter 2.]

WINDY: Fine. OK, let's have a look at that. Let's take these two
attitudes side-by-side, and you can tell me which explains the
visual pictures of you being bedridden. So, number 1 attitude
is: 'I really want a guarantee that, if I do all the right things, then
I have to have a guarantee that I'm going to be able to control
it.' In other words, 'I need to have a direct link between what
I do and the pain, and that's what has to be.' Or, 'I'd really like
to know that, if I do all the right things, then I'll be pain free,
but, given that I'm human, sadly it doesn't have to be that way
because human beings don't function that way.' Now which of
those two beliefs explains the bedridden, the first one or the
second?

ANAHITA: The first one, definitely.

WINDY: That's right. Now what image would you have of yourself if
you really believed the second one?

ANAHITA: … What emotion would I have?

WINDY: No, what image?

ANAHITA: What image would I have?

WINDY: Yeah. If you wouldn't see yourself as bedridden, how would
you see yourself?

ANAHITA: I find it difficult to get rid of the bedridden.

WINDY: No, because you just activated it. So, if you just let it be,
because you practise mindfulness, don't you?

ANAHITA: No.

WINDY: Oh, you practise yoga.

ANAHITA: Yeah. So then, if I strongly believed what I said …

WINDY: If you strongly believed the idea that, 'Look, I really would
like a guarantee that there's a direct link between what I do and
the pain, but, sadly, it doesn't have to be that way,' what image of

yourself do you have as opposed to, 'It's got to be that way and it would be terrible if it isn't'?

ANAHITA: Right, so I get a visual of me doing the best I can.

[Anahita can now see that there is not only a connection between her rigid attitude and the bedridden image but also a connection between her flexible attitude and having an image of doing the best that she can in the face of the adversity.]

WINDY: Right.

ANAHITA: ... Probably being very unhappy with further degeneration, should that happen, because I don't know.

WINDY: No, that's right.

ANAHITA: I'm assuming it's going to happen.

WINDY: Which attitude leads you to be more in control?

ANAHITA: Definitely the second one.

WINDY: So, isn't that interesting? You actually said that you feel out of control, and you're creating it, because you're actually believing that you have to have a guarantee of the direct link.

[Here I help Anahita to understand that her rigid attitude about having a guarantee of being in control actually helps to create her feeling of being out of control.]

ANAHITA: Yeah.

WINDY: So, can you see the relationship between you demanding, 'I've got to know for sure that, if I do this, that happens, and it's not happened – oh my God, I'm out of control, I'm bedridden,' as opposed to, 'Look, it'd be really nice, but I'm human, it doesn't have to be that way. I really want it,' and so you see yourself, still, realistically, maybe degenerating, but more in control.

ANAHITA: But what would I be in control of?

WINDY: What?

ANAHITA: Even as I say it, I'm wondering what I would be in control of, even if I acknowledge.

WINDY: Your emotional reactions to this.

[It is important that I stress that applying REBT can help Anahita with her anxiety. I am not claiming that REBT can directly help with her back pain. However, not being anxious may, and I stress may, have

a positive impact on the level of her pain, partly because she won't be focused on it as much.]

ANAHITA: Yeah.

WINDY: You see, because I'm not going to fall into the trap which says, 'REBT has a direct link to pain control relating to your back.'

ANAHITA: Yeah.

WINDY: Who knows? It may help because it might calm you down, and, when you've calmed down, it might. I don't know. But that's not what I'm saying. What I'm saying is would it help your anxiety?

ANAHITA: For sure.

WINDY: Right. So, do you have any reservations about giving up your need for the guarantee as opposed to still having the desire but really keeping that flexible?

ANAHITA: No. No reservations because I think, even if I keep it flexible, I will be on a regulated, disciplined routine. So, I don't fear that, if I give this up that I might indulge and be lazy.

WINDY: But also, given the fact that you're human, we know, when you're human, there's not a direct link, and something about being human means that we can't know for sure everything. One of the things about REBT is that it's based on a model of the human being which says we can know a lot about human beings but there are certain things which are not known and maybe unknowable.

ANAHITA: Right. Sometimes I think that's the scary bit.

WINDY: When you hold which attitude?

ANAHITA: When I hold the first attitude.

WINDY: Exactly. It's only scary when you kind of believe, 'No, I've got to know and, if I do this, I do that, and, if I do this and that doesn't work, oh, I'll be bedridden!' you see (said with humour)? That's how it works?

ANAHITA: Right.

WINDY: This visual representation of that.

ANAHITA: Yes.

WINDY: So there's something unknowable about this, and, if you have a healthy attitude, which is, 'Yeah, I really would like to know for sure, but I don't need to,' then you'll be more in control emotionally of not being in control of your pain.

ANAHITA: Yes, I do agree.

WINDY: Again, being human, what will happen, I think, realistically, probably, and I hope I'm wrong, the next time you notice that you're doing all the right things and your pain gets worse, you'll start becoming anxious again.

ANAHITA: Yes.

WINDY: At that point, what do you need to remind yourself of, in terms of what we've been talking about?

ANAHITA: ... [Pause] Maybe ... was I fooling myself? Well, there was no guarantee that doing all this would have 100% control the pain, number one. ... [Pause] And that it's really not the end of the world. Definitely, it isn't like I'm already bedridden, because, just because I get that visual, it's almost like I'm akin to bed-ridden right now, if I do that.

WINDY: Yeah.

ANAHITA: So, I can tell myself, well, I am doing x, y, z, maybe I'm not doing a to z, but ...

WINDY: 'And, when I have this image, then I'm actually rehearsing, unwittingly, my need for a guarantee of being able to have a direct link and to have that perfect control.'

ANAHITA: Right.

WINDY: Which then you can say, 'But I don't need that.'

ANAHITA: Yeah.

WINDY: 'I'd like it, but I don't need it.'

ANAHITA: Yeah.

WINDY: You see that's the important part.

ANAHITA: Yeah, and I'm probably at a level where I'd like it very, very, very, very, very much. That's where it is at.

WINDY: Yeah, indeed. Therefore, you'll have to work very, very, very, very, very hard to negate the 'must' bit; to say, 'No matter how much I really want it, sadly I still don't have to get it,' unless you think there's something special about you that says that, if you increase the 'verys', the powers that be have to grant you what you want.

[REBT has a realistic view of change. It argues that the more important a person's preference is, the more likely it is that they will make this preference rigid. But, and this is the realistic and, I would argue, optimistic point, the more important the preference, the harder the person needs to work to keep this preference flexible, but if they are prepared to do this work they can succeed at developing their flexible attitude.]

ANAHITA: Not at all.

WINDY: No? OK.

ANAHITA: I wish, but no.

WINDY: Yeah, and that may well be unfair, but that's the way it is.

ANAHITA: That's the way it is.

WINDY: It would be nice to have fairness in that respect, but do you need it or not?

ANAHITA: Yeah.

WINDY: Because, if you believe you need fairness, then you create another problem which is self-pity.

ANAHITA: Right, yeah.

WINDY: I'm not a specialist, but anxiety and self-pity may not be that great for your back.

ANAHITA: Yeah.

WINDY: Because both are burdens, and backs don't like burdens (said with humour).

ANAHITA: Sure.

WINDY: I'm not saying if you take off the burden that that's going to add, but I'm just thinking it might help you to unburden yourself emotionally and to see what happens with the back. OK?

ANAHITA: Sure, yeah.

Follow-up: seven months later[1]

A greater awareness of thinking choices and how I was 'doing myself in', better control over my feelings and a better sense of living in the present. This may briefly sum up how I felt after talking to Professor Dryden about the anxiety relating to my back problem. While being focused on my problem, he was also extremely humane, gentle yet firm, with a dry sense of humour – all of which I loved!

I learned the following (in the interview and reflecting on it after that too):

1. ***There are no guarantees that hard work will be rewarded with good outcomes.*** *That is, I can't **demand** that my back get better just because I'm working so hard on my fitness, diet and the like. However, it is sensible to keep my efforts going as it improves my overall fitness and health.*

How do I feel about that?

> On 'sensible-thinking' days, I'm unhappy about the lack of guarantees; I **wish** I had the guarantee of 'just' rewards, but don't **insist** on it. I remind myself that my demandingness runs counter to my goal of being concerned, and calm, and keeping my back in good shape. Consequently, if I miss a gym schedule due to a sore back, I do not hit the panic button. A notable change is that I haven't had disturbing images of me infirm, bedridden and enduring terrible suffering, as I was so prone to earlier.
>
> On 'unhelpful-thinking' days, I tend to brood awhile on the state of my back and whine about the loads of hard work that I have to do to keep my spine supple! On such days, I'm overly alert to the slightest unwanted niggle. Anxiety sets in. I have noticed, though, that the frequency and duration of these bad spells have vastly decreased. One out of ten days could be termed 'bad', as compared to four or five out of ten days, in the last couple of years.

2. ***My awfulising aggravates my pain.*** In my early days of medical treatment, my rheumatologist would emphasise each time I met him, that what needed re-working was my mind, not just my body. This would anger me, and I would insist that the bad back pain was ONLY a physical thing; was he implying that my pain was imaginary?

   Now, I understand how easily I work myself up to 'worse case scenarios'.

   I remind myself about my proneness to emotional reasoning and believing that the very existence of any kind of pain – even relatively minor – is VERY VERY VERY TERRIBLE. This helps me put the brakes, as it were, on my galloping negative thoughts.

3. ***Accepting the presence of pain is crucial.*** Earlier, I would fight the pain, insist in my head that it MUST vanish, and get increasingly disturbed if it didn't. I would swing between high hope on one day and hopelessness on the next. I would get extremely anxious, which would, in turn, exacerbate my pain.

   Talking to Professor Dryden helped in important ways. Now, I admit the fact that there is pain, that I am very very very unhappy about it and wish it were otherwise. I also try hard – and I find this very difficult in moments of pain – to reason with myself that ALL of life is not going to be bad despite the pain. I may miss out on some good times / good opportunities due to pain, which will be unfortunate, but I can still go on in life with reasonable *contentment. I use palliative methods too, like listening to music, reading, chatting with a friend or catching up on a Netflix serial to distract my attention from pain.*

Acceptance is easier understood in the head than implemented though! My efforts continue. In a longer session, I would have liked to have worked on this, with Professor Dryden.

4. ***Other things that have helped.*** *I feel greatly helped by these two quotes 1) Do the do-able. 2) Do what you can, with what you have, where you are. These help me set realistic goals and be easier on myself.*

Note

1   See Appendix 2 for the email I sent to volunteers requesting a follow-up.

Chapter 14

Reflections, summary and conclusion

In this final chapter, I will summarise and reflect on the conversations that I had with the 11 volunteers that appear in Chapters 3–13 and make a tentative conclusion. I will also discuss the feedback that the volunteers gave me on our conversations seven months after they took place. First, let me remind the reader of the theme of each conversation and its focus as shown in Table 14.1.

Three foci

It seems to be that the problems discussed by the volunteers in the published conversations can be grouped into three foci:

- Problems with an interpersonal / family focus
- Problems with an interpersonal / non-family focus and
- Problems with a non-interpersonal focus.

Let me now say a little more about each focus and the related conversations.

Problems with an interpersonal / family focus

In five of the 13 conversations that I had, the volunteer discussed a problem that could be said to focus on interpersonal issues with a member of their family. Three involved in-laws – Diya (3)[1], Em T (4) and Maia (5)[2] – one involved the person's son – Whisky (6) – and one tangentially involved the person's husband, but could be said to be an intrapersonal struggle – Megha (7).

Table 14.1 Volunteers, themes and the focus of the very brief therapeutic conversations

Name[3]	Chapter Number	Theme	Interpersonal / Family Focus	Interpersonal / Non-Family Focus	Non-Interpersonal Focus
Diya	3	Family Conflict	✓	x	x
Em T	4	Loss	✓	x	x
Maia	5	Lack of Influence and Involvement	✓	x	x
Whisky	6	Anxiety about Protecting Son	✓	x	x
Megha	7	Decision-Making about Giving Birth	(✓)	x	(✓)
Poorva	8	Inappropriate Behaviour	x	✓	x
M	9	Lack of Support	x	✓	x
Mrinmaye Sen	10	Disrespect	x	✓	x
Prats	11	Being Envied and Treated Unfairly	x	✓	x
Ananya	12	Dog Phobia	x	x	✓
Anahita	13	Physical Pain	x	x	✓

✓ = Definite indication
(✓) = Tentative indication
X = No indication

Problems with in-laws

Nowhere is the clash between traditional and modern values in India seen more starkly than in the relationships between husband and wife and their respective in-laws and this focus was present in three of the 13 conversations that I had.

Diya's (3) difficulties related not directly to her relationship with her in-laws but arose from the conflict between her parents and her in-laws who did not get on and refuse to meet with one another. Diya's anxiety centred on her in-laws 'bad-mouthing' her parents to her future children.

Em T (4) had been married for ten months when we had our conversation, and her difficulties were with two kinds of loss. She experienced a loss of autonomy as she was expected to spend every evening with her in-laws and to do things to which she silently objected. She also experienced a loss of connection with her parents with whom she felt 'at home'. She did not feel 'at home' in the marital home and was struggling with this.

As noted in endnote 2 of this chapter, Maia's (5) problems centred both on her lack of influence on how she wanted her sister to live her life and her lack of involvement in the planning of her sister's wedding. Although she was used to being the 'boy' in her family growing up, her sister is marrying into a traditional / patriarchal family, and she is not expected to have a say in the planning of the wedding. The clash between the traditional and the modern is quite apparent here.

Problem with son

Concerned mothers wanting the best for their sons, who see their 'good intentions' as nagging and an infringement on growing autonomy and who take little notice of them as a result, is a universal dynamic in family relationships. Whisky (6) is struggling with this dynamic and reports the common phenomenon of being damned with anxiety if she does nothing and damned with her son's sullen rebellion if she tries to get him to do what will help him to get what he says he wants.

Problem with husband and self

The conversation that I had with Megha (7) is difficult to classify as shown by my marking her problem with a tentative '(✓)' in two focus categories indicating my lack of sureness rather than a definite '√' in any one category. While her struggles with decision-making concerning where and how to give birth to her forthcoming baby relate to her husband, it perhaps more clearly relates to her own difficulties owning and expressing what are her very strong desires about the matter.

Problems with an interpersonal / non-family focus

When people wish to discuss interpersonal problems that do not have a family focus, usually they consider that they have been badly treated by other people. This was the case in the four conversations that had this focus. Thus, Poorva (8) had issues in the aftermath of being touched inappropriately by a male friend, M (9) considered that she was not supported by someone she came to regard as a surrogate father, Mrinmaye Sen (10) had an issue when treated with disrespect and Prats (11) struggled with being envied.

Problems with a non-interpersonal focus

Two of the volunteers wanted to discuss a problem that did not have an interpersonal focus. Thus, Ananya wanted help for dog phobia, and Anahita wanted help with psychological issues concerning physical pain.

The importance of discovering the volunteer's main adversity

My approach to VBTCs is based on the importance of making a focused assessment of the volunteer's problem. This helps me to go from the context in which the problem occurs to an understanding of what the person is mainly disturbed about within this context. This is known as the adversity at 'A' in REBT's 'ABC' framework (see Chapter 1). Table 14.2 summarises the volunteers' adversities as expressed in VBTCs. Identifying and working with each of the adversities listed in Table 14.2 enabled me to be precise about helping the volunteer to address their problem most effectively.

Table 14.2 **What volunteers regarded as adversities: a summary**

Name	Adversity
Diya (3)	Her parents-in-law may say derogatory things to her child about her parents
Em T (4)	She has lost autonomy in her life with her parents-in-law and has also lost the freedom she enjoyed while living with her parents
Maia (5)	Lack of influence over the way her sister lives her life and lack of involvement in the planning of her sister's wedding
Whisky (6)	Not discharging her protective function as mother so that her son does the 'right' thing
Megha (7)	Not wanting to be 'too demanding' about giving birth to her upcoming baby
Poorva (8)	Her actions contributing to the man who acted inappropriately towards her thinking that he can do what he wants
M (9)	Not being supported by the man she regarded as a surrogate father and him not explaining why
Mrinmaye Sen (10)	Being treated in a disrespectful manner
Prats (11)	Being envied and treated unfairly
Ananya (12)	Feeling fear around dogs
Anahita (13)	Not knowing for certain that she can control her pain if she does all the right things.

Dissatisfaction vs disturbance in VBTCs

Perhaps the most important contribution that REBT theory makes to my practice of VBTCs is its distinction between dissatisfaction and disturbance. Table 14.3 precisely summarises this distinction and the important factors involved.

As can be seen in Table 14.3, REBT theory holds that when people face an adversity at 'A', they have a choice to be dissatisfied about this adversity or disturbed about it. As I will presently discuss, a number of the volunteers thought that not being bothered about the adversity was a legitimate goal in dealing with it. The REBT-based riposte is that the only way that the person can achieve this is to

Table 14.3 **The distinction between dissatisfaction and disturbance in REBT**

A = <u>A</u>dversity	
B = Rigid and Extreme (<u>B</u>asic) Attitudes	B = Flexible and Non-Extreme (<u>B</u>asic) Attitudes
C = Disturbance (<u>C</u>onsequences of AxB)	C = Dissatisfaction (<u>C</u>onsequences of AxB)

lie to themself and pretend that it truly doesn't matter to them that the adversity exists. Such self-deception is not considered healthy in REBT. The fact that the volunteer had a problem with the adversity indicates that, if given a choice, the person would rather the adversity not happen. Such a statement reveals the person's preference which I want to incorporate in helping the person address the adversity as healthily as they can.

Broadly speaking, as Table 14.3 shows, when a person is faced with an adversity[4], and they hold a set of flexible and non-extreme attitudes towards that adversity, they will be dissatisfied that the adversity exists. Such dissatisfaction encourages the person to face the adversity, process it and change it if it can be changed or accept, but not like, it if it cannot be changed.

On the contrary, when a person is faced with the same adversity, and they hold a set of rigid and extreme attitudes towards it, they will be disturbed that the adversity exists. Such disturbance tends to prevent the person from facing the adversity, processing it and changing it if it can be changed or accept, but not like, it if it cannot be changed. Rather, it encourages the development of a range of strategies which unwittingly serve to perpetuate the person's problem.

Hence, one of my major strategies in VBTCs is to help the person to address their disturbance so that they can be healthily dissatisfied about the presence of the adversity as a prelude to addressing it effectively. Based on this central principle, let me summarise my conversations with the volunteers whose conversations with me were presented in Chapters 3–13.

Diya (3)

I helped Diya to recognise that her existence does not depend on her parents-in-law refraining from saying derogatory things about her parents to any children she may have in the future. This will help her to express her preferences to her in-laws and that such assertion is best underpinned by the idea that the latter do not have to comply with her wishes.

Em T (4)

I helped Em T to see that she can feel sad about the loss of her previous life and accept her mother-in-law as someone who will listen to her but who needed periodic reminders to do so. As a result, she does not have to rebel to maintain her autonomy. Rather she can accept, but not like, the status quo and exercise the more limited autonomy that she had in her present life which she was not exercising.

Maia (5)

I helped Maia to recognise that having a life script for her sister and wanting to be involved in the planning of her sister's wedding are legitimate desires, but that sadly and regretfully neither has to be met. Digesting these 'bitter pills' would help her a) to stay un-anxiously concerned and available to help her sister after her wedding and b) to recruit her mother to join forces with her to request greater involvement in the planning for that wedding with the groom's traditional family.

Whisky (6)

I helped Whisky to recognise that she does have a maternal responsibility which she could discharge flexibly or rigidly. Taking a rigid stance here only results in a nagging / non-listening pattern of interaction between them from which Whisky was keen to extricate herself. Being flexible means that she can encourage him to take responsibility for his decisions and be available to help should he request it. Such flexibility is also more likely to help her digest the point that life may be more successful in teaching her son the consequences of his actions than she may be.

Megha (7)

In my conversation with Megha, I mainly helped her to question her inference that having very strong child-bearing preferences and expressing them clearly to her husband means that she is being irrational and unfair on her husband. I did try to encourage Megha to assume that the latter inference was correct and identify and work with the rigid / extreme attitudes she held towards it, but Megha's response to this led me to abandon it and to work more inferentially with her. Interestingly, during the interview, Megha felt that I was supporting her in having and expressing very strong preferences and this led her to see that she could have a discussion with her husband during which she could be clear about how strongly she felt about the matter and state what she really wanted. My conversation with Megha shows that REBT therapists do not always have to work with attitudes and some-times working with inferences can lead to the person solving their problem. I think that this demonstrates the flexibility of REBT as a therapeutic approach and my flexible use of REBT (Dryden, 2018b).

Poorva (8)

Poorva held the rigid attitude that the man who behaved inappropri-ately with her in the past, an event which she says that she has dealt with, must not think that he can do what he wants to do and that holding on to her anger about the event prevents him from thinking this. I first helped Poorva to acknowledge that while it would be great if this man (and other men) did not have such thoughts, sadly and regretfully it does not follow that they must not think this way. At the end of the conversation, Poorva comes to see that holding the above flexible attitude and giving up her unhealthy anger does not mean that she is giving in or condoning such inappropriate male behaviour. Holding this flexible attitude also helps her to see that there is no connection between her felt anger and the man's thinking.

M (9)

I helped M to recognise that while it would have been highly prefer-able if her friend had supported her when others attacked her integ-rity at work and for him now to explain to her why he did not do so, she does not have to have either of her desires met. This flexible attitude would help her to persist to get an answer from him, but to accept but not like the fact that he may not do so.

Mrinmaye Sen (10)

Mrinmaye Sen struggled with feelings of unhealthy anger when she faced what she saw was disrespect from others. I helped her to develop a flexible attitude towards being disrespected from which base she could re-examine a number of unhelpful ideas she harboured about giving up her rigid demand towards this adversity.

Prats (11)

I helped Prats to acknowledge that while being envied and treated unfairly are undeserved adversities this does not mean that they must not happen to her. Holding this attitude would help her to assert herself with the people she mentioned who treated her in such a fashion.

Ananya (12)

I helped Ananya to see that addressing her dog phobia means that she needs to tolerate her fear and refrain from avoiding dogs when they approach her. I also helped her to see that the thought 'I'll die' stems from her rigid / extreme attitudes towards fear and that understanding this would allow her to have such a thought in her mind as she worked towards developing flexible / non-extreme attitudes towards fear.

Anahita (13)

Finally, I helped Anahita to develop the flexible attitude that while it would be highly desirable if there were a clear connection between doing all the right things for her back and a diminution of back pain to acceptable levels, sadly such a connection does not have to exist. Working towards holding such a flexible attitude would also help her to see that the image of being bedridden is largely created by the rigid version of her attitude and that she could develop a more realistic and functional image as her conviction in her flexible attitude grows.

Cognitive and behavioural change

Rational Emotive Behaviour Therapy is an approach that can best be placed within the cognitive-behavioural tradition of psychotherapy. As an REBT therapist, my objective is to help volunteers modify both their unconstructive thinking and behaviour. With respect to psychological change, REBT's preferred order is:

- First, change your basic attitude (at 'B') from rigid / extreme to flexible / non-extreme
- Then, change your behaviour (at 'C') and other forms of thinking (either at 'A' or at 'C').

As can be seen from the conversations presented, my main goal was to help the person to begin to make an attitudinal change. However, I also encouraged some volunteers to make other forms of cognitive change.

Cognitive change

As discussed in Chapter 1, when a person holds a rigid / extreme attitude towards an adversity, their subsequent thinking tends to be highly distorted and skewed towards the negative. Thus, Ananya (12) thinks that she will die if she gets bitten by a dog. Allowing for the fact that a small number of people do die from dog bites, this results from failing to get the appropriate injections afterwards, something I encourage Ananya to incorporate into her coping plan, and not from their anxiety. My main intervention concerning this cognitive consequence with Ananya was an educational one, helping her to see that it stems from her rigid / extreme attitude towards feeling anxious about dogs. As she says once she had begun to develop her new flexible / non-extreme attitude towards anxiety, the thought that she would die 'would not feature anywhere'.

I made a similar intervention with Anahita (13). She had a picture of herself bedridden with an achy back, and my conceptualisation was that this was a cognitive consequence of her previously expressed rigid attitude. When she developed her alternative flexible attitude, her new cognitive consequence of that attitude was that she saw herself doing the best that she could.

Behaviour change

One of the main points that I need to convey to volunteers when they find other people's behaviour problematic is the importance of changing their behaviour towards the other in order to promote behaviour change in the other. A good example of this is with Prats (11) where when she stays silent when others treat her unfairly, the result is that others think that he does not mind about how she is treated with the consequence that she receives more of such treatment. However, the reality is that she does mind about the other's behaviour and if she communicates this, it will encourage the other to change their behaviour in the desired direction.

REBT-based assertion

When asserting oneself to another person, I recommend that the person explicitly states the flexible attitude that underpins their behaviour. This occurs with Diya (3), Maia (5), M (9) and Prats (11). Here is an example with Maia (5): I say:

> Well, it depends, but, if you make a point of saying, and I do recommend this, 'Look, this is what I strongly want. You don't have to do it, but this is what I strongly want.' You express the idea that they don't have to do what you want, but you also express your preferences and the reasons for your preferences. Doing this keeps the idea alive that while one's desires don't have to be met, it is important to the person that they are met.

Other issues with training implications for REBT therapists

It should again be remembered that all the volunteers had had prior training in and exposure to REBT. Consequently, it may be thought that the conversations with me would reflect this fact. While this is the case in some respects, in other respects volunteers reveal a certain misunderstanding of REBT which have implications for the training of REBT therapists.

Difficulties with goals

REBT theory holds that since an adversity (at 'A') is a negative event for a person, it is productive for that person to experience a healthy negative emotion (HNE) and its behavioural and cognitive correlates (at 'B')[5]. As such, one might expect that volunteers who are knowledgeable about REBT should ideally set such HNEs as their adversity-related goals. This was not the case with M (9), Mrinmaye Sen (10) and Prats (11) who thought not being bothered about 'A' should be their goal – instantly in Mrinmaye Sen's case. It was also not the case with Whisky (6) who did not know what her goal should be.

Problems acknowledging and expressing very strong desires

Nowhere in REBT theory is it stressed that people should only have mild desires. Indeed, the theory encourages people to have and acknowledge both to themselves and others that their desires are very strong when this is the case. Maia (5) acknowledged to herself that her desires concerning being involved with the planning of her sister's wedding were strong, but had difficulty expressing these if they were not going to be met. Megha (7) had difficulty acknowledging and expressing her strong desires about where and how she wanted to give birth to her child because she thought that doing so would be demanding and unfair to her husband. Finally, Anahita (13) did not see clearly that as her preference for there being a direct link between her efforts and pain control was very strong that she had to work hard to keep this preference flexible.

Doubts, reservations and objections (DROs)

As I discussed in Chapter 2, people may have doubts, reservations and objections (DROs) to one or more aspects of the ideas that inform REBT practice as they experience them when in the helpee role. This was the case with Poorva (8) and Mrinmaye Sen (10). Poorva (8) thought that holding a flexible attitude towards a man thinking that it was OK for him to act inappropriately towards her meant that she was condoning such behaviour. Mrinmaye Sen (10) thought that her rigid attitude towards people respecting her was useful to her. For example, she thought that her rigid attitude helped her to be successful with people whereas on examination it was the preference component of this attitude and not its rigid component that helped her. As this preference component was also a part of her alternative flexible attitude, she could have the dual benefits of this attitude and none of the disbenefits of the rigid attitude.

Training implications

The previous comments show that it may be useful for REBT trainers to place more emphasis in training courses on the following:

- Healthy negative emotions stem from flexible / non-extreme attitudes towards adversity and that these can serve as clients' adversity-based goals.
- Desires can be very strong, and when this is the case, they are kept flexible when the person is clear that even their strong desires do not have to be met. However, the stronger a person's desire, the harder they may need to work to keep their attitude towards not having it met flexibly.
- People may have a range of idiosyncratic doubts, reservations and objections to REBT theory and practice and therapists need to inquire about these routinely.

Volunteer feedback

Seven months after the interviews, I wrote to each volunteer for feedback on the experience of the session and an update. Appendix 2 contains what I wrote to them. As noted earlier, volunteer feedback appears at the end of the interview, but what I want to do here is to offer some reflections about what the volunteers said.

Volunteer benefit

From the volunteer feedback, it appears that everyone got something constructive from the interview:

Diya (3)

Diya said that her problem "was resolved to a large extent."

Em T (4)

Em T said that "at an emotional level, I feel alleviated from the pain and way more accepting and forgiving towards my own self as against getting angry."

Maia (5)

Maia said that at moments she found it difficult to apply any learnings from the session and sometimes feels helpless, although going back to the recording and transcript helps her. Yet she also says that "by applying the same learning from the session ... I believe I am in a much better state to face my fears now".

Whisky (6)

Whisky noted that her problem was not solved, and neither was she expecting to solve it from one short session, but she said that "the session was definitely in the right direction." This testifies that for some a single session can help them make that forward step.

Incidentally, Whisky commented negatively on one aspect of the session[6]. She said, "The only drawback of the session I felt was that we had an audience and somewhere it was a little difficult to be very upfront and share and bare it all."

Megha (7)

Megha indicated that the session helped her as follows, "I got the birth I wanted, an unmedicated, natural birthing experience and it was life-changing". She went on to say that "the feeling that I am asking for too much still persists even now, but now I know how to help myself with it".

Poorva (8)

Poorva said, "my problem got solved very much during the session. I don't see myself having the problem anymore".

M (9)

M said, "the problem doesn't seem to trouble me to the extent it did earlier".

Mrinmaye Sen (10)

Mrinmaye Sen said:

> I solved my problem after the one on one brief therapy with Prof. Dryden, and after a few months, I realised that such similar triggers were not bothering me as much. In fact, a few weeks back a similar trigger occurred, but I was able to get over the problem very quickly ...

Prats (11)

Prats said, "I have solved my issues to a great extent after the session. I am at peace, and I definitely can't control how others think about me, but I can definitely control my reaction to the problem".

Ananya (12)

While still wary of dogs, Ananya said that she is much less frightened of them and while she related an episode where she called for help, this experience did not stop her from going for a run straight afterwards which was her presenting problem.

Anahita (13)

Writing about dealing with her anxiety about her back pain, Anahita said:

I have noticed, though, that the frequency and duration of these bad spells have vastly decreased. One out of ten days could be termed 'bad', as compared to four or five out of ten days, in the last couple of years.

Use of recording / transcript

As mentioned in Chapter 2, when I have a very brief therapeutic conversation with a volunteer, I routinely record the VBTC and offer the person the recording and later a written transcript of the session. I do ask the person to contact me to request these materials which are sent to them at no charge. I do not have a record of how many of the 11 volunteers requested the recording / transcript. However, three people referred to these resources in their feedback.

Maia (5)

Maia was one of a few of the volunteers who struggled with the same problem after the conversation. It is in this context that she refers to the recording and transcript. Thus, Maia said:

Honestly, there were few moments when I found it difficult to apply any of the learnings attained during the session. But, I kept going back to the transcripts and recordings of the session to remind me what I forget – avoid making my strong desires to rigid attitudes.

Even today, I get the same anxiety-provoking thoughts. I feel helpless. But going back to the learnings from the sessions I had with Prof. Dryden, helps me get back to the moment.

Prats (11)

Prats provided general positive views about her use of the materials. She said, "I did request the recording and transcript of the session, and it's been useful introspection and for dealing with other cases".

Ananya (12)

Ananya referred to her use of the recording in addressing her fear of dogs. She said, "the recording of the session was very helpful because

I would play it and listen to it often, especially before going for my run, and that helped me focus on my run to a great extent."

Comments

I am surprised that more of the volunteers did not mention using the recording and / or the transcript of the conversation. It is not known how many requested the materials, and of those who did request them, only three referred to their use in their feedback. The use of such resources after VBTCs needs more scrutiny.

Of the two volunteers who discussed how they specifically employed the materials, both seemed to use them to try to convince themselves of something that they were finding hard to digest. It is as if they cannot internalise something and they are going back to the recording or transcript in the hope of finally doing so. At a follow-up session, this would be explored, but no such follow-up was possible.

Feedback on my contributions

Many volunteers referred to my contributions to our very brief thera-peutic conversation. This can be divided into my technical REBT-based contributions and my more general relational contributions. I will treat them separately here, although, of course, these two types of contributions interact in therapeutic practice.

What the volunteers said about my technical contributions

By technical contribution here, I mean that which relates specific-ally to my practice of REBT in the 'tasks' and 'views' domain of the working alliance (Bordin, 1979; Dryden, 2006, 2011) as opposed to the more general relational contribution which refers more to the 'bonds' domain of the alliance. Thus in this section, I will con-sider what mention volunteers made of my interventions and what I helped them to understand about their problem and how they could tackle them, both from an REBT perspective.

DIYA (3)

Diya mentioned that I helped her to identify her own inherent auto-matic thought pattern. She said that I directed her:

in a manner which felt as if I could easily and naturally correct or change that thought, not making it sound as if it is impossible or difficult to stop feeling the anxiety. In fact, his style of session felt as if it was simple to make the change in my thinking and behaviour.

EM T (4)

Em T said that she "did have awareness in the root cause of the problem but what struck the most with me was the ease with which Professor Dryden hit the nail on the head and tied it to 'loss' – loss of autonomy". Here, Em T is referring to my practice of taking time to identify the volunteer's personalistic adversity at 'A' in the ABC framework. She also said that I helped her "to accept the undesirable change in myself which I abhorred, with more compassion".

MAIA (5)

Maia said that the:

> session was a strong reminder for me that my loved ones have choices just like I do. I can certainly express my strong desires, in their best interest, but I need to remember not to allow them to transform into demands from them.

WHISKY (6)

Whisky did not provide any feedback on my technical contribution but did comment on my relational contribution (see later).

MEGHA (7)

Megha mentioned that I asked her "important and pertinent questions to understand who or what was standing in my way to solve ... [her] ... problem". She seemed to feel that my questions and the frame that I put them in helped her to conclude that she had "the right to wish for the kind of birthing I wanted." Megha also referred to the 'teach your children' technique that I used to help her see that she could teach her new child that they can have any strength of desire and to express it. Megha shows that what she learned is that she can have very strong desires and not be demanding.

POORVA (8)

Poorva said, "Dr Dryden's choice of words during the session and his accurate analysis of the problem (which I thought I was aware of until he guided me to it) was his most helpful contribution to the session".

M (9)

M said that "the interview aptly focused on my needs and helped me gain clarity towards the solutions I was seeking ... and [he] ... helped me look into the matter with different perspectives."

MRINMAYE SEN (10)

Mrinmaye Sen stated that I helped her by confirming with her exactly which disturbance to work on and by helping her see that when things do not happen according to her wish then this cannot lead to neutral feelings. She understood that one will always have a negative feeling about situations that are important and don't conform to the person's expectations.

PRATS (11)

Prats said that I "played a very important role in making me realise that I can't control the way others think and I can't make everyone happy". I also helped her to learn "the art of expressing my thoughts and opinions to the other person without hurting them".

ANANYA (12)

Ananya said:

> what I liked most about the interview was that the assessment evaluated and addressed all the irrational beliefs, and also the secondary emotional problem. In addition, it also gave me an insight into how I actually have a plan of action, in case I got bitten by dogs.

ANAHITA (13)

Anahita initially said that I helped her gain "a greater awareness of thinking choices and how I was 'doing myself in', better control over my feelings and a better sense of living in the present." She said that I also helped her to see i) that there are no guarantees that hard work will be rewarded with good outcomes; ii) awfulising aggravates pain and iii) accepting the presence of pain is crucial.

What the volunteers said about my relational contributions

In this section, I will consider the mention that volunteers made of my relational contributions to the conversations session in the 'bonds' domain of the working alliance (Bordin, 1979; Dryden, 2006, 2011).

DIYA (3)

Diya mentioned the ease with which I worked and how simple I made the ideas we discussed.

EM T (4)

Em T also mentioned the ease with which I helped her to identify her adversity at 'A'. The smoothness of therapeutic interaction is an important feature of the therapeutic bond.

MAIA (5)

Maia was one of three volunteers who referred to my use of humour when she pointed to, "the jovial manner in which he struck the chords of simple common sense".

WHISKY (6)

I mentioned earlier that Whisky was the only volunteer who did not refer to my technical contribution in her feedback, but she did mention my relational contribution. She said:

> I found Professor Dryden very attentive, paying attention to minor details and very empathetic. This approach encouraged

me to relax and be able to talk more and more freely about my most secretive thoughts. Despite there being a time limit, I did not feel rushed or hurried. Adequate attention was paid to my feelings and my responses. Professor Dryden's body language was one of deep involvement.

She also mentioned that I created a therapeutic climate where "there was no right or wrong. It was about each person's own views and perspectives. There was no blame game".

MEGHA (7)

Megha stated that "the deep respect and acceptance I felt of me, and my problem was itself very healing ... I marvel at the fact that in just those 15–20 minutes, my situation was understood deeply and accurately".

Of all the volunteers, perhaps my conversation with Megha (7) had the deepest impact. She concludes her feedback thus:

> Thank you, Windy, for your help. You played a huge and important role in supporting me in having the birth experience of my choice. My baby got the best and healthiest kind of beginning to his life because you helped me believe that it was ok that it was very very very very very important to me and that I could communicate it in that manner. I'll always be deeply grateful to you for that.

POORVA (8)

In her discussion of my technical contribution (see earlier), Poorva referred to my use of words, especially 'sadly and unfortunately', which helped to make her flexible attitude more palatable. Here she mentions that these words validated her feelings. She says that my "validation of feelings using the words 'sadly and unfortunately it doesn't have to be so', will almost always stay with me". This example perhaps more than any other shows how the relational and technical contributions work hand-in-hand to yield a memorable intervention.

M (9)

M referred to the effortlessness of my demonstration of the therapeutic process which is another example of 'interactional smoothness' mentioned by Diya (3), Em T (4) and Whisky (6). She mentioned feeling very comfortable all through the session.

MRINMAYE SEN (10)

Mrinmaye Sen mentioned my lucidity and understanding.

PRATS (11)

Prats did not mention my relational contribution in her feedback but did refer to my technical contribution (see earlier).

ANANYA (12)

Ananya referring to me said, "it was amazing how he built the therapeutic alliance so quickly and beautifully. His ability to use humour also made my session a lot of fun, and it helped me look at my problem from a different perspective."

ANAHITA (13)

Anahita, again referring to me said, "while being focused on my problem, he was also extremely humane, gentle yet firm, with a dry sense of humour – all of which I loved!"

Summary

Tables 14.4 and 14.5 provide summaries of the feedback that volunteers gave of my technical and relational contributions to our conversations. All but one volunteer (Whisky-6) provided feedback about my technical contributions and all but one (Prats-11) provided feedback on my relational contributions.

Looking at Table 14.4, it can be seen that 20 separate pieces of technical feedback were provided by the volunteers. Eight pieces of feedback related to specific issues concerning REBT theory and practice (shown in italics), while 12 were expressed in more general

Table 14.4 **Volunteer feedback on my technical contributions to the conversations: summary (n = 20)**

My Technical Contributions
• Helped to identify my inherent automatic thought pattern (Diya-3)
• *Helped to identify the adversity at 'A' (Em T-4)*
• *Helped me to accept the undesirable change in myself which I abhorred, with more compassion* (Em T-4)
• Reminded that my loved ones have choices (Maia-5)
• *Helped to see that I can express my desires without transforming them into demands* (Maia-5)
• Helped to identify blocks to solving the problem (Megha-7)
• *Helped to conclude that I can have very strong desires* (Megha-7)
• Analysed my problem accurately (Poorva-8)
• *Choice of words helped me to digest flexible attitude towards others not respecting boundaries* (Poorva-8)
• Provided clarity towards the solutions I was seeking (M-9)
• Provided different perspectives (M-9)
• Helped to focus me on the right problem to work on (Mrinmaye Sen-10)
• *Stressed the healthiness of healthy negative emotions [HNEs]* (Mrinmaye Sen-10)
• Helped me realise that I can't control the thoughts and feelings of others (Prats-11)
• Helped me to learn the art of expressing my thoughts and opinions to the other person without hurting them (Prats-11)
• *Addressed all my irrational beliefs and my secondary emotional problem* (Ananya-12)
• Helped me gain a greater awareness of thinking choices and how I was 'doing myself in' (Anahita-13)
• Helped me gain better control over my feelings (Anahita-13)
• Helped me gain a better sense of living in the present (Anahita-13)
• *Helped me learn a) there are no guarantees that hard work will be rewarded with good outcomes; b) awfulising aggravates pain and c) accepting the presence of pain is crucial* (Anahita-13)
NB Italicised items are specific to the theory and practice of REBT (n = 8)
Non-italicised items are more general in nature (n = 12)

Table 14.5 **Volunteer feedback on my relational contributions to the conversations: summary (n = 18)**

• Interactional ease / unhurried / felt comfortable x 4 (Diya-3; Em T-4; Whisky-6; M-9)
• Humour x 3 (Maia-5; Ananya-12; Anahita-13)
• Empathetic / Understanding x 3 (Whisky-6; Megha-7; Mrinmaye Sen (10)
• Attentiveness (Whisky-6)
• Body language was of deep involvement (Whisky-6)
• Deep respect (Megha-7)
• Acceptance (Megha-7)
• Validation of feelings (Poova-8)
• Lucidity (Mrinmaye Sen-10)
• Humane (Anahita-13)
• Gentle, but firm (Anahita-13)

terms. This is the case even though most volunteers were REBT trainees. It is interesting therefore to note that such a group of people experiences the technical part of the conversation in general ways even when the conversations were heavily influenced by REBT.

Looking at Table 14.5, it can be seen that 18 separate pieces of feedback were provided by the volunteers about my relational contribution to the conversations. A variety of relational factors were mentioned, the most common being what I have called 'interactional smoothness', a sense that the volunteers have of being engaged in an easy and effortless conversation. This was mentioned by four people. Two factors that were each mentioned by three people were empathy / understanding and humour. The rest of the factors in Table 14.5 were each mentioned once, perhaps showing my relational range during the conversations.

Taken together, Tables 14.4 and 14.5 show how intertwined such technical and relational factors are in therapeutic conversations. Any attempt to highlight one set of factors over the other will give only half the story about REBT, even though it has a lot of technical features.

Generalisation

Generalisation refers to the case where a volunteer takes the learning that they derived from discussing their chosen problem with me and applies this learning to other areas of their life. Seven of the 11 volunteers mentioned that they did (or are doing) this in their written feedback.

Generalisation to a deeper version of the problem

MAIA (5)

Maia looked more into the problem that she discussed with me and applied the same learning she derived from the conversation to a deeper version of the problem.

Generalisation more widely

Three volunteers generalised their learning more widely than their presenting problem.

MEGHA (7)

Thus, Megha stated:

> So now, when I have a wish, I check it on the scale of one to five 'very / s', which puts a lot of things in perspective for me. It has helped me in communicating my wishes so much easier because I now have clarity on how important that particular wish is to me.

POORVA (8)

Poorva said, "I am actively trying to work on my demands of fairness from people in general".

PRATS (11)

Finally, Prats speaking of "the art of expressing my thoughts and opinions to the other person without hurting them", said, "I am using this principle in dealing with all my issues after that session".

Helping clients

Two volunteers mentioned using what they learned from the conversation in their work as a therapist.

DIYA (3)

Thus, Diya said:

> As a practitioner of REBT, I learnt the ease with which one can make the client realise his own inner thought pattern. And help them with behavioural change without aggressively telling them what to do. So not only I learnt how to apply it to myself but also with my clients.

MRINMAYE SEN (10)

Having learned the importance of healthy negative emotions to the resolution of the problem that she discussed with me, Mrinmaye Sen stated, "Now in my private practice, I encourage my clients not to hope for neutral feelings towards subjects of importance but work towards acceptance of healthy negative feelings".

Helping a friend

EM T (4)

Finally, reflecting on her conversation with me that centred on dealing with the loss of autonomy, Em T said, "I helped another friend who went through a similar phase make sense out of her distress".

Conclusion

My aim in this book has been to show that Rational Emotive Behaviour Therapy (REBT) can be used very briefly with people who wish for help for problems of daily living. However, such an effect could ultimately have only come about if the volunteers applied what they learned from the conversations to their everyday life. In almost all cases, this occurred, and in some cases, learning was generalised to other problems and to the person's own work as a therapist. All this from a conversation that lasted 25 minutes, and in many cases, less. It is my fervent hope that such brief interventions can be routinely made available at the point of need rather than at the point of availability. When this occurs, people may benefit so that they can get on with their lives free from the needless disturbance and pain that are suffered by many even in problems of daily living.

This brings us to the end of this book. I hope you have found it instructive and I welcome any feedback sent to me at windy@windydryden.com.

Notes

1   When I discuss a volunteer in this chapter, the number in brackets refers to the chapter number in which the conversation I had with them can be found.
2   Maia (5) discusses two linked problems in her conversation with me, both relate to her sister. The first concerns how Maia wants her sister to live her life and the second relates to the difficulties she has with family of the man her sister plans to marry.
3   Each volunteer provided a name by which they wanted to be known in this book. They all provided a release form agreeing to have their conversation included and discussed by me in this book.
4   As discussed more fully in Chapter 2, my REBT-influenced approach to VBTCs is predicated on the position that, initially, the volunteer is asked to assume, temporarily, that the adversity (at 'A') that features in the problem is true. Doing so helps us both to identify the rigid / extreme attitudes that underpin the person's disturbed response to the adversity and to develop the flexible / non-extreme attitudes that serve to underpin the person's healthy response to the same adversity. Helping the person to change 'A' instead may relieve the person of their disturbed feelings, but does not help them to develop the aforementioned flexible / non-extreme attitudes should the person encounter 'A' in the future.
5   See Chapter 1 and Appendix 1.
6   This was the only negative piece of feedback given by any of the volunteers.

A guide to the eight emotional problems and their healthy alternatives with adversities, basic attitudes and associated behaviour and thinking

Anxiety vs concern

Adversity	• *You are facing a threat to your personal domain*	
Basic Attitude	**Rigid and Extreme**	**Flexible and Non-Extreme**
Emotion	**Anxiety**	**Concern**
Behaviour	• You avoid the threat • You withdraw physically from the threat • You ward off the threat (e.g. by rituals or superstitious behaviour) • You try to neutralise the threat (e.g. by being nice to people of whom you are afraid) • You distract yourself from the threat by engaging in other activity • You keep checking on the current status of the threat hoping to find that it has disappeared or become benign • You seek reassurance from others that the threat is benign • You seek support from others so that if the threat happens they will handle it or be there to rescue you • You over-prepare in order to minimise the threat happening or so that you are prepared to meet it (NB it is the over-preparation that is the problem here)	• You face up to the threat without using any safety-seeking measures • You take constructive action to deal with the threat • You seek support from others to help you face up to the threat and then take constructive action by yourself rather than rely on them to handle it for you or to be there to rescue you • You prepare to meet the threat but do not over-prepare

	• You tranquillise your feelings so that you don't think about the threat • You overcompensate for feeling vulnerable by seeking out an even greater threat to prove to yourself that you can cope		
Subsequent thinking	*Threat-exaggerated thinking* • You overestimate the probability of the threat occurring • You underestimate your ability to cope with the threat • You ruminate about the threat • You create an even more negative threat in your mind • You magnify the negative consequences of the threat and minimise its positive consequences • You have more task-irrelevant thoughts than in concern	• You are realistic about the probability of the threat occurring • You view the threat realistically • You realistically appraise your ability to cope with the threat • You think about what to do concerning dealing with the threat constructively rather than ruminate about the threat • You have more task-relevant thoughts than in anxiety • You picture yourself dealing with the threat in a realistic way	
	Safety-seeking thinking • You withdraw mentally from the threat • You try to persuade yourself that the threat is not imminent and that you are 'imagining' it • You think in ways designed to reassure yourself that the threat is benign or if not, that its consequences will be insignificant • You distract yourself from the threat e.g. by focusing on mental scenes of safety and well-being • You over-prepare mentally in order to minimise the threat happening or so that you are prepared to meet it (NB once again it is the over-preparation that is the problem here) • You picture yourself dealing with the threat in a masterful way • You overcompensate for your feeling of vulnerability by picturing yourself dealing effectively with an even bigger threat.		

Depression vs sadness

Adversity	• You have experienced a loss from the sociotropic and / or autonomous realms of your personal domain • You have experienced failure within the sociotropic and / or autonomous realms of your personal domain • You or others have experienced an undeserved plight	
Basic Attitude	**Rigid and Extreme**	**Flexible and Non-Extreme**
Emotion	**Depression**	**Sadness**
Behaviour	• You become overly dependent on and seek to cling to others (particularly in sociotropic depression) • You bemoan your fate or that of others to anyone who will listen (particularly in pity-based depression) • You create an environment consistent with your depressed feelings • You attempt to terminate feelings of depression in self-destructive ways • You either push away attempts to comfort you (in autonomous depression) or use such comfort to reinforce your dependency (in sociotropic depression) or your self- or other-pity (in pity-based depression)	• You seek out reinforcements after a period of mourning (particularly when your inferential theme is loss) • You create an environment inconsistent with depressed feelings • You express your feelings about the loss, failure or undeserved plight and talk in a non-complaining way about these feelings to significant others • You allow yourself to be comforted in a way that helps you to express your feelings of sadness and mourn your loss
Subsequent thinking	• You see only negative aspects of the loss, failure or undeserved plight • You think of other losses, failures and undeserved plights that you (and in the case of the latter, others) have experienced • You think you are unable to help yourself (helplessness) • You only see pain and blackness in the future (hopelessness) • You see yourself being totally dependent on others (in autonomous depression) • You see yourself as being disconnected from others (in sociotropic depression) • You see the world as full of undeservedness and unfairness (in plight-based depression) • You tend to ruminate concerning the source of your depression and its consequences	• You are able to recognise both negative and positive aspects of the loss or failure • You think you are able to help yourself • You look to the future with hope

Guilt vs remorse

Adversity	• You have broken your moral code • You have failed to live up to your moral code • You have hurt someone's feelings	
Basic Attitude	**Rigid and Extreme**	**Flexible and Non-Extreme**
Emotion	**Guilt**	**Remorse**
Behaviour	• You escape from the unhealthy pain of guilt in self-defeating ways • You beg forgiveness from the person you have wronged • You promise unrealistically that you will not 'sin' again • You punish yourself physically or by deprivation • You defensively disclaim responsibility for wrongdoing • You make excuses for your behaviour • You reject offers of forgiveness	• You face up to the healthy pain that accompanies the realisation that you have sinned • You ask, but do not beg, for forgiveness • You understand the reasons for your wrongdoing and act on your understanding • You atone for the sin by taking a penalty • You make appropriate amends • You do not make excuses for your behaviour or enact other defensive behaviour • You accept offers for forgiveness
Subsequent thinking	• You conclude that you have definitely committed the sin • You assume more personal responsibility than the situation warrants • You assign far less responsibility to others than is warranted • You dismiss possible mitigating factors for your behaviour • You only see your behaviour in a guilt-related context and fail to put it into an overall context • You think that you will receive retribution	• You take into account all relevant data when judging whether or not you have 'sinned' • You assume an appropriate level of personal responsibility • You assign an appropriate level of responsibility to others • You take into account mitigating factors • You put your behaviour into overall context • You think you may be penalised rather than receive retribution

Shame vs disappointment

Adversity	• Something highly negative has been revealed about you (or about a group with whom you identify) by yourself or by others • You have acted in a way that falls very short of your ideal • Others look down on or shun you (or a group with whom you identify) or think that they do	
Basic Attitude	**Rigid and Extreme**	**Flexible and Non-Extreme**
Emotion	**Shame**	**Disappointment**
Behaviour	• You remove yourself from the 'gaze' of others • You isolate yourself from others • You save face by attacking other(s) who have 'shamed' you • You defend your threatened self-esteem in self-defeating ways • You ignore attempts by others to restore social equilibrium	• You continue to participate actively in social interaction • You respond positively to attempts of others to restore social equilibrium
Subsequent thinking	• You overestimate the negativity of the information revealed • You overestimate the likelihood that the judging group will notice or be interested in the information • You overestimate the degree of disapproval you (or your reference group) will receive • You overestimate how long any disapproval will last	• You see the information revealed in a compassionate self-accepting context • You are realistic about the likelihood that the judging group will notice or be interested in the information revealed • You are realistic about the degree of disapproval self (or reference group) will receive • You are realistic about how long any disapproval will last

Hurt vs sorrow

Adversity	• Others treat you badly (and you think you do not deserve such treatment) • You think that the other person has devalued your relationship (i.e. someone indicates that their relationship with you is less important to them than the relationship is to you)	
Basic Attitude	**Rigid and Extreme**	**Flexible and Non-Extreme**
Emotion	**Hurt**	**Sorrow**
Behaviour	• You stop communicating with the other person • You sulk and make obvious you feel hurt without disclosing details of the matter • You indirectly criticise or punish the other person for their offence • You tell others how badly you have been treated, but don't take any responsibility for any contribution you may have made to this	• You communicate your feelings to the other directly • You request that the other person acts in a fairer manner towards you • You discuss the situation with others in a balanced way, focusing on the way you have been treated and taking responsibility for any contribution you may have made to this
Subsequent thinking	• You overestimate the unfairness of the other person's behaviour • You think that the other person does not care for you or is indifferent to you • You see yourself as alone, uncared for or misunderstood • You tend to think of past 'hurts' • You think that the other person has to make the first move to you and you dismiss the possibility of making the first move towards that person	• You are realistic about the degree of unfairness in the other person's behaviour • You think that the other person has acted badly rather than as demonstrating lack of caring or indifference • You see yourself as being in a poor situation, but still connected to, cared for by and understood by others not directly involved in the situation • If you think of past hurts you do so with less frequency and less intensity than when you feel hurt • You are open to the idea of making the first move towards the other person

Problematic anger vs non-problematic anger

Adversity	• You think that you have been frustrated in some way or your movement towards an important goal has been obstructed in some way • Someone has treated you badly • Someone has transgressed one of your personal rules • You have transgressed one of your own personal rules • Someone or something has threatened your self-esteem or disrespected you	
Basic Attitude	**Rigid and Extreme**	**Flexible and Non-Extreme**
Emotion	**Problematic Anger**	**Non-Problematic Anger**
Behaviour	• You attack the other(s) physically • You attack the other(s) verbally • You attack the other(s) passive-aggressively • You displace the attack on to another person, animal or object • You withdraw aggressively • You recruit allies against the other(s)	• You assert yourself with the other(s) • You request, but do not demand, behavioural change from the other(s) • You leave an unsatisfactory situation non-aggressively after taking steps to deal with it
Subsequent thinking	• You overestimate the extent to which the other(s) acted deliberately • You see malicious intent in the motives of the other(s) • You see yourself as definitely right and the other(s) as definitely wrong • You are unable to see the point of view of the other(s) • You plot to exact revenge • You ruminate about the other's behaviour and imagine coming out on top	• You think that the other(s) may have acted deliberately, but you also recognise that this may not have been the case • You are able to see the point of view of the other(s) • You have fleeting, rather than sustained thoughts to exact revenge • You think that other(s) may have had malicious intent in their motives, but you also recognise that this may not have been the case • You think that you are probably rather than definitely right and the other(s) as probably rather than definitely wrong

Problematic jealousy vs non-problematic jealousy (or relationship concern)

Adversity	• A threat is posed to your relationship with your partner from a third person	
	• A threat is posed by uncertainty you face concerning your partner's whereabouts, behaviour or thinking in the context of the first threat	
Basic Attitude	**Rigid and Extreme**	**Flexible and Non-Extreme**
Emotion	**Problematic Jealousy**	**Non-Problematic Jealousy (Relationship Concern)**
Behaviour	• You seek constant reassurance that you are loved • You monitor the actions and feelings of your partner • You search for evidence that your partner is involved with someone else • You attempt to restrict the movements or activities of your partner • You set tests which your partner has to pass • You retaliate for your partner's presumed infidelity • You sulk	• You allow your partner to initiate expressing love for you without prompting him / her or seeking reassurance once s / he has done so • You allow your partner freedom without monitoring his / her feelings, actions and whereabouts • You allow your partner to show natural interest in members of the opposite sex without setting tests • You communicate your concern for your relationship in an open and non-blaming manner
Subsequent thinking	• You exaggerate any threat to your relationship that does exist • You think the loss of your relationship is imminent • You misconstrue your partner's ordinary conversations with relevant others as having romantic or sexual connotations • You construct visual images of your partner's infidelity	• You tend not to exaggerate any threat to your relationship that does exist • You do not misconstrue ordinary conversations between your partner and another man / woman • You do not construct visual images of your partner's infidelity • You accept that your partner will find others attractive but you do not see this as a threat

Problematic envy vs non-problematic envy

Adversity	• Another person possesses and enjoys something desirable that you do not have	
Basic Attitude	**Rigid and Extreme**	**Flexible and Non-Extreme**
Emotion	**Problematic Envy**	**Non-Problematic Envy**
Behaviour	• You disparage verbally the person who has the desired possession to others • You disparage verbally the desired possession to others • If you had the chance you would take away the desired possession from the other (either so that you will have it or that the other is deprived of it) • If you had the chance you would spoil or destroy the desired possession so that the other person does not have it	• You strive to obtain the desired possession if it is truly what you want
Subsequent thinking	• You tend to denigrate in your mind the value of the desired possession and / or the person who possesses it • You try to convince yourself that you are happy with your possessions (although you are not) • You think about how to acquire the desired possession regardless of its usefulness • You think about how to deprive the other person of the desired possession	• You honestly admit to yourself that you desire the desired possession • You are honest with yourself if you are not happy with your possessions, rather than defensively trying to convince yourself that you are happy with them when you are not • You think about how to obtain the desired possession because you desire it for healthy reasons • You can allow the other person to have and enjoy the desired possession without denigrating that person or the possession • You think about what the other has and lacks and what you have and lack

Email to volunteers asking for feedback

Seven months after the conversation

I would be grateful if you could provide a written account of your experiences of the interview and what happened subsequently. This will appear in the book at the end of the chapter in which our session appears.

While I don't want to be prescriptive and I want you to write what you want in your own way, you might find the following points and questions useful in writing your contribution:

- Please describe your experience of the interview. What did you like about it and not like about it?
- What did you learn from the session?
- Did you solve your problem after the session? To what extent do you still have the problem?
- What use, if any, did you make of what you learned in your life subsequent to the session?
- Did you apply what you learned to other areas of your life? If so, please explain.
- Please describe Professor Dryden's role in the session. What was helpful and not helpful about his contribution to the session?
- If you requested the recording and transcript of the session, what use did you make of them?

References

Beck, A.T. (1976). *Cognitive therapy and the emotional disorders.* New York: International Universities Press.

Bordin, E.S. (1979). The generalizability of the psychoanalytic concept of the working alliance. *Psychotherapy: Theory, Research and Practice, 16,* 252–260.

Colman, A. (2015) *Oxford dictionary of psychology.* 4th edn. Oxford: Oxford University Press.

David, D., Cotet, C., Matu, S., Mogoase, C. & Stefan, S. (2018). 50 years of rational-emotive and cognitive-behavioral therapy: A systematic review and meta-analysis. *Journal of Clinical Psychology, 74,* 304–318.

Davis III, T.E., Ollendick, T.H. & Öst, L-G. (Eds.). (2012). *Intensive one-session treatment of specific phobias.* New York: Springer.

Dryden, W. (Ed.). (1989). *Howard Young – rational therapist: Seminal papers in rational-emotive therapy.* London: Gale Centre Publications.

Dryden, W. (1996). *Overcoming anger: When anger helps and when it hurts.* London: Sheldon Press.

Dryden, W. (2001). *Reason to change: A rational emotive behaviour therapy (REBT) workbook.* Hove, East Sussex: Brunner-Routledge.

Dryden, W. (2006). *Counselling in a nutshell.* London: Sage.

Dryden, W. (2011). *Counselling in a nutshell.* 2nd edn. London: Sage.

Dryden, W. (2013). *The ABCs of REBT: Perspectives on conceptualization.* New York: Springer.

Dryden, W. (2016). *Attitudes in rational emotive behaviour therapy: Components, characteristics and adversity related consequences.* London: Rationality Publications.

Dryden, W. (2018a). *Very brief therapeutic conversations.* Abingdon, Oxon: Routledge.

Dryden, W. (2018b). *Flexibility-based cognitive-behaviour therapy: Insights from 40 years of practice.* Abingdon, Oxon: Routledge.

Dryden, W. (2019). *Single-session therapy; 100 key points and techniques.* Abingdon, Oxon: Routledge.

Ellis, A. (1963). Toward a more precise definition of "emotional" and "intellectual" insight. *Psychological Reports*, *13*, 125–126.

Ellis, A. (1994). *Reason and emotion in psychotherapy*. Revised and updated edition. New York: Birch Lane Press.

Ellis, A. & Joffe Ellis, D. (2011). *Rational Emotive Behavior Therapy*. Washington, DC: American Psychological Association.

Epictetus (1983). *The handbook*. (N.P. White, Trans.). Indianapolis, IN: Hackett.

Hauck, P.A. (1991). RET and the assertive process. In M.E. Bernard (Ed.), *Using rational-emotive therapy effectively: A practitioner's guide* (pp. 197–218). New York: Plenum.

Hoyt, M.F., Bobele, M., Slive, A., Young, J. & Talmon, M. (Eds.). (2018). *Single-session therapy by walk-in or appointment: Administrative, clinical, and supervisory aspects of one-at-a time services*. New York: Routledge.

Hoyt, M.F. & Talmon, M. (Eds.). (2014). *Capturing the moment: Single session therapy and walk-in Services*. Bethel, CT: Crown House Publishing Ltd.

Joshi, A. & Phadke, K.M. (2018). *Rational emotive behaviour therapy integrated*. New Delhi: Sage.

Keller, G. & Papasan, J. (2012). *The one thing: The surprisingly simple truth behind extraordinary results*. Austin, TX: Bard Press.

Kellogg, S. (2015). *Transformational chairwork: Using psychotherapeutic dialogues in clinical practice*. Lanham, MD: Rowman & Littlefield.

Matweychuk, W.J. & Dryden, W. (2017). *Rational emotive behaviour therapy: A newcomer's guide*. Abingdon, Oxon: Routledge.

Maultsby, M.C. Jr. (1975). *Help yourself to happiness: Through rational self-counseling*. New York: Albert Ellis Institute.

Miller, W.R. & C'de Baca, J. (2001). *Quantum change: When epiphanies and sudden insights transform ordinary lives*. New York: Guilford Press.

Persons, J.B. (2008). *The case formulation approach to cognitive-behavior therapy*. New York: Guilford Press.

Talmon, M. (1990). *Single session therapy: Maximising the effect of the first (and often only) therapeutic encounter*. San Francisco, CA: Jossey-Bass.

Tangney, J.P. (1995). Shame and guilt in interpersonal relationships. In J.P. Tangney & K.W. Fischer (Eds.), *Self-conscious emotions: The psychology of shame, guilt, embarrassment, and pride* (pp. 114–139). New York, NY: Guilford Press.

Index

For Product Safety Concerns and Information please contact our EU
representative GPSR@taylorandfrancis.com
Taylor & Francis Verlag GmbH, Kaufingerstraße 24, 80331 München, Germany

www.ingramcontent.com/pod-product-compliance
Lightning Source LLC
Chambersburg PA
CBHW062022270326
41929CB00014B/2283